Right and Wrong Expectations in Friendship

Right and Wrong Expectations in Friendship

by
Don Clowers

Harrison House
Tulsa, Oklahoma

Right and Wrong Expectations in Friendship
ISBN 1-57794-348-1
Copyright © 2000 by Don Clowers
Don Clowers Ministries
P.O. Box 3168
Coppell, Texas 75019

Published by Harrison House, Inc.
P.O. Box 35035
Tulsa, Oklahoma 74153

Dedication

To Nelson Patterson,
preacher par excellence and best friend.

I heard Nelson preach his first message when he was eleven years old. He was present the night I fully dedicated my life to God. Had he not been there that night, I really don't know if I would have made that dedication. But God put him in my path, so I did make it.

Nelson heard me preach my first message when I was fifteen years old. Although he was only twenty-one months older than I was, he had been saved longer than I, and he preached with such power that I looked up to him. My respect for him caused me to listen carefully to his instruction as he helped me in my Christian walk.

From our teens onward, Nelson and I did most things together. We double-dated together, we prayed all night together, we preached together, we visited the sick together, we traveled together, we pastored together, we took time off together and we laughed together.

I had more fun with Nelson than with anybody else I'd ever been around. We had such a good relationship that no matter what challenge came to our friendship, we were always able to work through it. He was a great influence in my life, and I will be eternally grateful for what he gave me. He trusted and believed in me; he challenged me.

Then the time came for Nelson to look to me for support. In 1989 I watched a tumor eat away and finally consume his life. I prayed with him and talked to him almost daily during this trial. Now he suffers no more, and he walks with Jesus every day.

Thank you, Nelson, for the confidence you had in me. I was so saddened by your passing from this life. No one but God knows how much I miss you. You are still a part of me. You invested so much of yourself in me, and much of who I am is because of you.

Contents

Foreword: Why Are Relationships So Important?

Acknowledgments

Introduction

PART I: DEVELOP A FRIENDLY LIFESTYLE

1 Be Friendly...25

2 Nurture a Real Interest in Others...............29

3 Focus on the Strengths of the Individual 32

4 Treat All People as Equals.........................34

5 Make Your Friends Feel Special 37

6 Trust Your Friends 39

7 Pray With Your Friends.............................41

8 Be There in Triumph and Tragedy 44

9 Allow Your Friends To Grow 48

10 Demand Nothing in Return 50

11 Show Gratitude 52

PART II: FIX YOURSELF FIRST

12 Know Who You Are..................................61

13 Find Out Who You Truly Are and Be
That Person 65

14 Live Close to God in Your Heart 70

15   Avoid Seeking the Approval of Others 73

16   Get Into the Relationship for the Right Reason 75

17   Ask Yourself: Why Am I Getting Involved? 77

18   Build Up the Altar, Not the Problem.........................81

PART III: COMMUNICATE, COMMUNICATE, COMMUNICATE

19   Discuss Any Offenses With Your Friends
     Early and Often as Needed 87

20   Deal With Issues, Don't Run From Them 93

21   Admit Your Errors 96

22   Find an Answer Before You Point
     Out the Problem 97

23   Discover What Your Friends Think
     of Themselves...99

PART IV: TIP IN ADVANCE

24   Be Careful With Labels; People Tend To
     Live Up to Them..103

25   Treat the Person Right and Give All That
     You've Got...110

26   Learn To Tip in Advance...113

PART V: LEARN THE DIFFERENCE BETWEEN GIVING AND RECEIVING

27   Once You Give, It's No Longer Yours........................119

28   Understand the Principles of Giving.........................123

PART VI: CONTROL YOUR EXPECTATIONS

29   Don't Expect Gratitude...137

30   Don't Keep Score..151

31   Control Your Expectations......................................154

32   Dealing With Unfulfilled Expectations.....................161

33   Risk Friendship..165

PART VII: GUARD YOUR EMOTIONS

34 Submit Your Emotions to God.................................169

35 Don't Let Friends Upset You.................................175

36 Respond in Love; Don't React in Anger.....................177

37 Give No Place to the Devil.................................182

38 Insecure People Treat You the Way They
    See Themselves...185

39 Hurting People Hurt People.................................192

40 Overlook Faults...198

41 Overcome Discouragement, Disillusionment
    and Deception..201

42 Never Leave a Relationship Offended......................211

43 Grieving Inordinately Is Holding Onto
    Something You No Longer Have...........................218

PART VIII: AVOID RELATIONSHIPS THAT KILL

44 Selfishness...223

45 Self-Pity...225

46 Fear of Rejection...230

47 Pride, Arrogance and an Overbearing Manner.........237

PART IX: STRENGTHEN YOUR RELATIONSHIP WITH GOD AND THE CHURCH

48 Yield to the Spirit of God................................245

49 Deal With Unresolved Issues...............................248

50 Lay Yourself and Your Ambitions on the Altar.........263

PART X: RECOGNIZE AND TREASURE A GOOD RELATIONSHIP

51 How To Recognize and Treasure a
    Good Relationship......................................269

Foreword

Why Are Relationships So Important?

Have you ever noticed that people are everywhere you go these days, and most of them don't do things the way you would like to have them done? There was a time in my life when I continually noticed this type of thing, and actually, most of the people I encountered aggravated me! But I am happy to say that I really don't pay much attention to how different everyone is from me now, and I don't expect them to give me my happiness in life. This change in my attitude has set me free to enjoy people, and therefore, to enjoy life.

Did you ever stop to realize that you cannot enjoy life if you don't enjoy people? How many people are you around much of the time whom you don't enjoy? If those people never change, does that mean you will never be able to enjoy your life? If you have that attitude, you are in the same boat I was, and *you need a new attitude about relationships.*

This superior book on right and wrong expectations was written by a man who has a tremendous gift for developing good relationships. Don Clowers is a personal friend as well as a co-laborer with me in the ministry. I can truly say that I have learned a great deal about relationships from being around Don and his wife, Sharon. They are a good example of what they teach. I believe this book will bring multiplied thousands into healthier relationships.

Did you know that the Bible is a book about relationships? It is about our relationship with God, with ourselves and with other people. These are three distinct relationships, but they must all be healthy for life to flow properly. Much of the New Testament is about church life and the relationships of the believers, which applies to us as believers today, with other believers, with unbelievers, with those in authority over us and with those under our authority. It covers the husband and wife relationship, the parent and child relationship and the employer and employee relationship. The Bible tells us how we should treat those weaker than we are, as well as our neighbors and those who are in need, and it also covers the way we should treat every other type of relationship we may have.

Because the Word of God places such an emphasis on relationships, I feel we must do the same; therefore, I believe this book is a very important one and should be read by every person who wants to grow in having better relationships.

The things that Don shares about right and wrong expectations are particularly interesting to me. I believe this insight sheds much needed light on why so many people seem easily offended. Offense has become a big problem, even in the church, and it greatly hinders the flow of the anointing, which is vital to our seeing lives change. The anointing comes where there is unity, not strife and offense. We expect all kinds of things from people who don't even know we are expecting something, and therefore, they often fail to meet our expectations.

I recently read an estimate that stated 50 percent of first marriages[1] and 60 percent of second marriages[2] now end in divorce. I have also read that, sad to say, born-again Christians are slightly more likely than non-Christians to divorce[3]—*something is wrong!* I think we expect people to do for us what only God can and should be expected to do. There are some things that we have a right to expect from other people, and there are some things that we don't have a right to expect. I believe this excellent book will help each reader find balance and move into peaceful and joyful relationships with the variety of people they encounter in life.

I highly recommend this book for immediate reading.

—*Joyce Meyer*
Bible Teacher, Conference Host and Author

Acknowledgments

I have been in the ministry since I was fifteen years old. During that time, God has blessed me with some precious relationships. He's brought people into my life to love me and stand beside me in good times and bad. The man I am today is the result of many of the long-term relationships that have helped mold and fashion me over the years. I will be eternally grateful for those people who have been special to me in my work for God.

My family is especially a dear part of my life. My precious mother, for example, who is now in the presence of God, prayed for me and taught me the ways of God. My dad displayed so much godly character, and he taught me how to develop my own character. My brothers and sister, who have loved me, are very dear to me too.

My wonderful, loving wife, Sharon, has suffered many hardships without complaining and has stood firmly for God in the midst of great adversity. She is steady, faithful and always loving. Next to my relationship with God, my relationship with my wife has been the greatest one of my life. I thank God for giving me a wife who could be so understanding and generous to her children, the ministry and me. Sharon, I love you so much. Thank you for all you have given me.

My beautiful daughter, Tammy, was so terribly injured when hit by a car, but through God's grace and healing power she was spared from death. She has been such a delight to her mother and me. I could never thank her enough for all she's meant to me.

My son David means so much to me too. He has accepted God's call on his life and is seeking to please Him with all of his heart. The times we spend just talking make me proud to have the opportunity to know a person as fine as he is. David means more to me than anyone could ever know. I enjoy spending time with him and watching him grow in God.

My son Tim has such a good personality, and I love him with such fervor. He is unique and very special. Like his brother David, he has also accepted the call of God. I love to just sit with him and listen to him talk. Our relationship has blossomed, and I feel very close to him. I see much of myself in him. Every minute we are together is a wonderful experience. Now I am so blessed to see him in full-time ministry.

My son Jeff is now in heaven. I have missed him very much, but knowing that he's in God's presence eases the pain. When he was alive, he was so thoughtful and caring. His kindness blessed many, and those he touched will always remember him. I will always cherish his last day, when he and I had lunch together. It was such a great time of fellowship. Then a few minutes later he was with the Lord. He had so much depth in his life. He was so good and kind, and he always loved me, just as I loved him. Our relationship was awesome.

I thank the Lord for the opportunity to have known, loved and be loved by all of these true friends.

Introduction

We all experience some things in life that bring us great joy and other things that hurt us deeply. No one likes to be hurt, but our response to the things that hurt us will determine whether we become bitter or better. Some people get bitter after being hurt; others become better. Usually, our expectations are at the root of each response and determine which outcome we will produce.

For example, we've all found ourselves waiting for people who promised to meet us somewhere at a certain time but were late. That can be very frustrating, but it can also be a great opportunity to develop godly patience.

Have you ever found yourself in a particularly frustrating situation like this? Of course. We all have. If you happen to be waiting for some friends to arrive, for example, and they don't show up, you begin to get worried. You expect them to be there. Every time you hear a noise, you think they've arrived. You may begin listening for the car to pull into the driveway, or go to the window to watch for them. Or you try to keep the telephone close by, expecting them to call. If one of your teenage children or your spouse makes a phone call, for example, you ask them to free up the line for your friends to call. Why do you do this? Because you're in a state of expectation.

Being in a state of expectation is being ready for something to happen. But what happens when that something doesn't happen?

Have you thought about the times you yourself have perhaps raised and then dashed another person's expectations? Perhaps you gave someone a reason to expect something but then you didn't follow through. Perhaps you promised something that didn't mean as much to you as it did to the other person. Or perhaps you were halfhearted when you made a comment, but the other person took your comments seriously. While making conversation, maybe you said, "Let's get together for lunch or dinner." The other person may have thought you were making plans and expected a firm commitment, when all you were doing was expressing a general desire to get together at some future date.

People get disappointed in these types of situations because their levels of expectation have been raised. And people with raised levels of expectation can understandably become disappointed.

Many times I've had to forgive people who raised my expectations by saying they were going to call or make plans with me but never did. Now, it's up to me to get over it, but sometimes it's not so easy.

A lot of people make commitments and then change their minds when it comes time to follow through. Let's face it. Some people are just fickle.

Perhaps it is we who have changed our minds at the last minute. We should examine ourselves. If we expect others to trust and respect us, we must keep our word.

Jesus talked plainly about this subject, **Say only yes if you mean yes, and no if you mean no. If you say more than yes or no, it is from the Evil One** (Matt. 5:37 NCV).

This book is not about living up to the expectations of others or about what is right or wrong with others. This book is about how to live our lives respectfully and how to treat others when we have been wronged or think we have been wronged. It is about trying to do what is right, regardless of what someone else is doing.

In difficult situations in dealing with others, I have found that my attitude is more important than the facts. If I maintain the right attitude, I can better deal with the facts. A wrong attitude or motive can cause me to miss the plan that God has for me. Furthermore, a wrong attitude can damage my relationships with others.

Good relationships are wonderful and make life sweeter. I would not have enjoyed so many great experiences had it not been for my friends who were there to enrich the moment, teaching me about life or introducing me to things that made my life better.

On the other hand, I've been hurt by friends and felt betrayed by people I trusted, while expecting unanswered promises. This is the risk involved in relationships.

Other times I was the one who caused the hurt. Because of my immaturity or because I placed unrealistic expectations on others, I felt let down. Perhaps I wasn't being as sensitive to the needs of others as I could have been.

Sometimes it's hard to know just how a person is feeling. But, regardless of who let down whom, I've tried to learn from each experience—whether good or bad—so that I can be wiser and better informed. And as I learn from my mistakes, I can live in peace and trust people more.

Since life is so short, we need to live each day in peace and in the presence of God, learning to appreciate the people God places in our lives. Among the friends God gives us to know, some may turn out to be friends for a season, while others may become friends for life.

I believe there are friends who are supposed to be a part of our lives but are prevented from doing so for unforeseen reasons. For example, David and Jonathan in the Bible, though the best of friends, were kept apart by King Saul's jealousy and hatred of David.

After David had finished talking with Saul, he met Jonathan, the king's son. There was an immediate bond of love between them, and they became the best of friends. (Sam. 18:1.)

Saul, however, boiled with rage. *You fool!*" he yelled at Jonathan. "Do you think I don't know that you want this son of a nobody to be king in your place, shaming yourself and your mother? As long as that fellow is alive, you'll never be king. Now go and get him so I can kill him!"

"But what has he done?" Jonathan demanded. "Why should he be put to death?"

Then Saul hurled his spear at Jonathan, intending to kill him. It was then that Jonathan realized his father really wanted David dead! Jonathan left Saul in fierce anger and refused to eat all that day. He was hurt by his father's shameful behavior toward David. (1 Sam. 20:30-34 TLB.)

Things happen over which we have no control. We must realize that decisions made by others sometimes affect our relationships and our lives. These decisions may hurt us, but we have basically two ways to respond: We can hold on to the wrong, or we can forgive and move forward. Looking back at the hurt is destructive both to ourselves and to others, so the better choice of the two is to forgive and look to the future.

One way to know whether or not we've forgiven someone is to examine ourselves for the presence of resentment or pain. When we no longer experience those feelings when thinking about the person who wronged us, we know we've been healed. When we remember the good times more than we remember the bad, we know that a healing has occurred. That doesn't mean we need to keep the person who hurt us close by, but we do need to move on to a place where that person no longer negatively dominates our thoughts.

It is my desire to help people grow in their relationships, both with God and with others. In this book I will share principles I've learned in my relationships so those experiences in turn can encourage you to pursue healthy relationships for yourself. Hopefully, it can also pinpoint areas where you may still need to grow.

I count it a great honor to have been called into a ministry in which I have the opportunity to reach people all over the world. As you read this book with an open heart and mind, I pray it will minister to you too.

If you find yourself hurting because of a bad experience in a relationship, I pray you will first mend yourself by making sure you are right with God. If you have been treated wrongly in the past, I pray you will set yourself free by forgiving, and allow God to show you the green pastures of His love. David acknowledged that only God can do this: **You will show me the way of life, granting me the joy of your presence and the pleasures of living with you forever** (Ps. 16:11 NLT).

Therefore, let's take a look at what makes a good relationship and explore how you can enrich others as you are enriched yourself.

PART I

Develop a Friendly Lifestyle

Chapter 1

Be Friendly

Our society isn't very big on developing healthy friendships. Most people think of friends as people to spend time with when there's nobody else around. Others think of friends as people with whom they can network for their advantage in business. Still others may think of friends as people they can count on to help them out during personal emergencies.

But ask any of us what it means to really have a friend, and we would probably echo the words of John Lyly, who described a friend as a "pleasure in prosperity, a solace in adversity, a comfort in grief, a merry companion in joy, and at all other times 'another I.'"[1]

Yet, in reality, we speak less and less of friendship and more and more of relationships. Perhaps the two are the same, with the difference being only a shift in our language over the years. Or perhaps relationships are really the first step toward true godly friendships.

You see, God desires for us to experience a holy intimacy, a connection and a true friendship with others. For instance, He shows us examples of steadfast friendships throughout the Bible, such as David's friendship with Jonathan.

The Bible is full of portrayals of relationships—even relationships that went awry and ended in betrayal, such as Judas' betrayal of Jesus. More importantly, the Bible also teaches us that when we love one another, people will recognize us as being Jesus' disciples. (John 13:35.)

One of the most compelling Scriptures regarding friendship is Proverbs 18:24, which says, **A man that hath friends must shew himself friendly.** Showing oneself friendly is much more than practicing superficial acts, such as smiling and laughing at other people's jokes. True, smiling and having a good sense of humor are important, but showing oneself friendly means so much more. It means developing a friendly lifestyle.

By showing ourselves friendly, we practice being nice when we don't feel like being nice. It means giving when we don't feel like giving. It means acting with civility even when we don't feel like it. Showing ourselves friendly also means preventing unimportant disagreements to rupture our important relationships, thereby causing arguments and broken friendships.

I heard a story once—whether it is true or not, I don't know—but I like the story because it illustrates a very important principle. As the story goes, a couple once got into a trivial argument that eventually led to their divorce.

The husband said to his wife one day, "Why did you burn these biscuits?"

She said, "I *didn't* burn the biscuits."

"You *did* burn the biscuits," he insisted.

"I *did not* burn the biscuits."

This argument caused a bit of a rift, which escalated into a major rupture and eventually led to the end of their marriage.

Some time after the divorce, the two of them were talking, and one of them admitted, "You know, it was really silly to get divorced over such an unimportant argument." The other agreed, and they reconciled, got healed emotionally and remarried.

Some months later, this couple was sitting at the same table when that old subject of those biscuits came up. The husband said, "That really was stupid for us to get divorced over your burning the biscuits, wasn't it?"

"I *didn't* burn the biscuits," she said.

"You *did* burn the biscuits," he argued.

"I *did not* burn the biscuits."

They soon found themselves in another big argument over the same stupid biscuits!

How many times have we rehashed trivial things as this couple did and robbed ourselves of good relationships?

Showing oneself friendly means preventing a relationship from being ruptured by unimportant disagreements.

Showing oneself friendly also means accepting one another as we are, without trying to change each other. It means being patient and kind, finding a way to be constructive, rejoicing when right and truth prevail and always believing in one another.

Furthermore, showing oneself friendly means not being anxious to impress someone else. It involves ridding ourselves of such negative qualities as jealousy, boastfulness, arrogance, rudeness, bad manners, self-interest, irritability, resentfulness, touchiness and the tendency to gloat over another's failures.

Showing oneself friendly is more than a pretty smile and a friendly hello. The act of showing oneself friendly means getting out of one's self-absorbtion and developing a lifestyle with a genuine loving attitude, as outlined in the love chapter, 1 Corinthians 13:4-8.[2]

Chapter 2

Nurture a Real Interest in Others

To make a deliberate and conscious effort to nurture a real interest in others[1], celebrate their victories and commit to really listening is a tough but rewarding challenge. Despite the rewards of nurturing others, it may be easier to close people off and push them away.

When we push people away, however, we think we won't have to deal with their problems and their needs. But in pushing them away, we are actually pushing ourselves away. And the joy we could experience in life by sharing godly friendships is lost. It takes courage to stick it out with someone through hard times, but the rewards usually far outweigh the risk.

I am reminded of an article written many years ago about a primitive tribe of people who wore portraits of themselves on their foreheads. When they confronted one another, they bowed to the *image* of the other person rather than to the person. That is a picture of what we do when we treat good friends superficially, avoiding a real interest in them.

Sometimes it's easier to avoid a real interest in others, especially when you have a friend who loves to talk about himself. Have you ever had a friend who always tops your story of success with one of his or her own?

Story-topping may feel good to the story-topper at the moment, but nurturing a real interest in others means really hearing what *they* have to say. It is important to listen with respect, concern and a genuine feeling of understanding.

Harvey MacKay, in his book *Swim with the Sharks Without Being Eaten Alive,* stresses the importance of nurturing a real interest in others as a practice of doing good business with others. He suggests a sixty-six-question customer profile that covers the standard Rolodex questions but moves into more personal questions later. For example, he suggests asking about education, family, business background, special interests, lifestyle and relationships with others.

MacKay's profile covers questions that most of us have never even asked our closest friends.

A few of these questions are as follows:

- What schools did you attend?
- If you didn't attend college, do you want to?
- What is your opinion on being in the service?
- What are your children's interests?
- What are your greatest concerns in life at this time?
- On what topics of interest do you have strong feelings?
- What do you like to read?
- What are your long-range personal goals in life?[2]

Unfortunately, people in business often recognize the value of nurturing people more than friends do. As sad as that may seem for us today, I don't think it has always been that way. There was a time in this country when interpersonal relationships were of paramount importance. Generally, I think it has been easier for many of us to seek economic growth instead of personal growth.

As a country in general, we have lost a rich heritage. I think we lost a sense of commitment in the sixties, our closeness to others in the seventies and much of our spirituality in the eighties. But it's not too late to get all of these values back. One way to rediscover them, I believe, is to stretch out our hands to one another with real interest and love, seeking to really know one another better.

Once we've cultivated a real interest in others, we can genuinely celebrate their victories as well as our own. We have espoused our own interests long enough. Now is the time to rejoice with someone else when he or she wins, achieves or overcomes something.

Finally, we must commit ourselves to listening to others. Really listening. Too often we only pretend to be hearing those around us. We stand in a listening position and tilt our heads just so—even look people in the eyes—but many times our minds are racing forward to our own thoughts and the responses we want to make. When this happens it is we, not they, who are the losers.

The German dramatist and novelist, Suderman, who stripped away the pretenses of the middle-class society in the late 1800s said, "I know how to listen when clever men are talking. That is the secret of what you call my influence."[3]

Any influence we may expect to have with our friends is won or lost on the listening field. Until someone trusts us to truly listen, we have not yet established a relationship; we have made only an acquaintance.

Chapter 3

Focus on the Strengths of the Individual

When we focus on our friends' strengths instead of their weaknesses, we give them room to grow. They may possess brilliant talents that heavy-handedness could destroy. In *The Good Natured Man*, Oliver Goldsmith observed, "We must touch [our friends'] weaknesses with a delicate hand. There are some faults so nearly allied to excellence, that we can scarce weed out the fault without eradicating the virtue."[1]

In the Bible, Euodias and Syntyche worked side by side with the apostle Paul in Philippi, telling others the Good News of Jesus Christ. But when something happened that caused a quarrel between them, they began to focus on the other's faults and weaknesses instead of on their strengths. Apparently, this break in relationship became a crisis. We know this because Paul wrote to the pastor of the church, pleading for the reconciliation of friendship between these two. In fact, in Philippians, Paul addresses Euodias and Syntyche and the leadership of the church to implore them to restore their relationship:

> **Always be full of joy in the Lord; I say it again, rejoice! Let everyone see that you are unselfish and considerate in all you do. Remember that the Lord is coming soon. Don't worry about anything; instead,**

pray about everything; tell God your needs and don't forget to thank him for his answers. If you do this you will experience God's peace, which is far more wonderful than the human mind can understand. His peace will keep your thoughts and your hearts quiet and at rest as you trust in Christ Jesus.

And now, brothers, as I close this letter let me say this one more thing: Fix your thoughts on what is true and good and right. Think about things that are pure and lovely, and dwell on the fine, good things in others. Think about all you can praise God for and be glad about. Keep putting into practice all you learned from me and saw me doing, and the God of peace will be with you.

Philippians 4:4-9 TLB

We are all aware that none of us is perfect—yet despite our faults, we all have strengths. Some of our strengths may even border on brilliance or genius. But we cannot develop those gifts if we are continually being criticized. We need room to try out the talents and gifts God has given us. We need room to discover these gifts and explore them without fear of others pointing out our faults. That's why it's so important to focus on one another's strengths instead of one another's weaknesses.

Chapter 4

Treat All
People
as Equals

Admittedly, it can be very hard to accept people just as they are and respond to them honestly when we are aware of their shortcomings. It can be even harder to accept others as equals without reserving a small sense of superiority over them in one area or another. After all, they may not have our experience, background, knowledge or understanding of the things we've lived through.

However, when we harbor this judgmental kind of attitude, we proceed to build lopsided relationships, favoring our own perspectives.

Consequently, we never get to fully experience the other people's true values. Maintaining a judgmental attitude toward others prevents us from hearing what they are really saying to us. It also prevents us from seeing the strength of character or greatness of talent that lies within them.

Pride and haughtiness blind us to the real virtues people possess. And if we smugly compare our friends to ourselves, we further alienate them because of a false sense of superiority. For example, we may think we are wiser, stronger or better in every way. We may think the brands of clothes we buy are the absolute best. Or we may think our decisions are the only correct ones.

We might also point out—with alacrity—why their choices are inferior to ours.

This is wrong. The truth is that every one of us has strengths and weaknesses. In actuality, we might be surprised to find out what superior talents our friends possess in certain areas. We should not be so full of ourselves that we overlook or underestimate others' strengths.

Philippians tells us that the first step to seeing others as equals is to learn to esteem them as better than ourselves:

> **Don't be selfish; don't live to make a good impression on others. Be humble, thinking of others as better than yourself. Don't just think about your own affairs, but be interested in others too, and in what they are doing.**
>
> **Your attitude should be the kind that was shown us by Jesus Christ, who, though he was God, did not demand and cling to his rights as God, but laid aside his mighty power and glory, taking the disguise of a slave and becoming like men. And he humbled himself even further, going so far as actually to die a criminal's death on a cross.**
>
> **Yet it was because of this that God raised him up to the heights of heaven and gave him a name which is above every other name.**
>
> **Philippians 2:3-9 TLB**

The more you begin to practice this attitude of godliness, the more you will be a good friend to others. Romans 12:10 tlb urges us to prefer one another in honor: **Don't just pretend that you love others: really love them. Hate what is wrong. Stand on** the side of the good. **Love each other with brotherly affection and take delight in honoring each other.**

We treat others as equals when we respect their opinions, experience, knowledge, time, space and privacy. Too often, however, we demonstrate our attitudes toward others by invading their privacy. For example, we take a peek at their mail, read documents on their desks (upside down, of course!) or rudely interrupt them. Or we treat their space—be it personal, office or home—as though we have the right to trespass and use it without permission. We make them feel inferior when we take up too much of their time and seem unconcerned about their schedules. This sometimes happens when we drop by their office to chat, or demand attention when we know their schedule is packed. Would we tolerate such behavior from others toward ourselves? Of course not!

We disrespect others when we continually consider our own time to be more important than theirs. Our knowledge, experience and opinions are certainly not necessarily superior to theirs. It is unreasonable to expect that any one of us is always totally accurate, or more well-read or more up-to-date on the current research in our field.

There is so much we can learn from others when we treat them as equals. Each person you meet has a unique viewpoint, perspective and interpretation of life. Find out what those are. The sharing of this knowledge will expand and enrich your life.

Chapter 5

Make Your Friends Feel Special

Let your friends occupy a special place in your life. Of course you should never let friends take precedence over God and family, but you should let them know how special they are to you. Your friends are important to you, and they should know that. Despite your harried schedule, take some time to be with your friends, showing them that you don't think of them as minor annoyances, but rather as important people who deserve some of your time.

With so many relationships disintegrating around me, I get the feeling we as a society aren't cherishing friendships or making our friends feel special enough. I constantly search for ways to enrich my friendships. Over the years, I have discovered five ways that I believe make friends feel more special, and I want to share them with you.

The first way to make your friends feel special, of course, is to make time for them. When you take time to fit your friends into your busy schedule—refusing to preempt them for other things—you gain joy from it. Making your fellowship times together significant will also make your friends feel special.

A second way of making your friends feel special is to genuinely care about them. Be conscious of their joys and pains, highs and lows, successes and failures; and respond to them in an appropriate and caring manner.

The third way of making your friends feel important is to tear down any walls that make them feel distanced from you. Work on sharing intimately with them. Share your thoughts, your dreams and your goals with them. By letting them into your life like this, you will find that you are enriching your friendships. However, don't expect your friends to always like what they find. A true friend will be honest with you despite what he or she hears. And though it may sometimes be difficult for you to be vulnerable, with the right friends, you can be, and you will always be better for the experience.

Pray for your friends regularly. Be open with them and disclose your feelings honestly—even your struggles, your joys and your hurts. Learn to be honest with them in a sensitive and civil manner. By displaying sensitivity to their needs while maintaining their confidences, your relationships will grow and flourish. Remember to always be accountable to them and to also hold them accountable.[1]

The fourth way to make friends feel special is to choose to be committed to them. Love them unconditionally, even though you may not agree with all of their opinions. Whatever resources you have to offer them—time, energy, insight—should be available to them.

The fifth way to make your friends feel special is to show them that you trust them. Samuel Johnson, in *The Rambler*, said, "It is better to suffer wrong than to do it, and happier to be sometimes cheated than not to trust."[2] Trust is the atmosphere in which any relationship grows and develops. Once trust is gone, it is difficult to rebuild.

Chapter 6

Trust Your Friends

Trust must be present in any relationship before there can be true intimacy. Trust must first come from within; it is an internal virtue that emanates outward. Behaviors can mislead us, but the internal virtues of being faithful, caring, honest, dependable and loyal are the bedrock of trust.

Trust is not a virtue that is automatically present in a relationship. Rather, it is a quality developed gradually over time. Trust must be nurtured. In *The Secret of Loving*, Josh McDowell writes, "I believe trustworthiness is simply a reflection of what we are like deep down inside and what we have proved ourselves to be. And it takes time to build this quality into our character."[1]

As good friends, we are proven trustworthy over time by choosing to be faithful, caring, honest, dependable and loyal. Each day we are faced with thousands of choices, most of which are small ones that seem insignificant. However, sometimes we make the kinds of choices that lead to the question, *Who would know if I did something I think no one will see?* Ironically, the answer to that question is often that many people will know.

All of our small choices help determine our character—what we are like deep down inside—and none of us can hide his or her character for long, whether good or bad.

Given enough time, people read us fairly accurately, discovering, almost unerringly, who we are. Then we wonder why people sometimes respond to us differently than we expect them to. It is because they have read our characters and have concluded how much or how little they can trust us.

When people don't trust us, they probably won't tell us to our faces, but their actions will reveal it.

We have the power to change all that, no matter what our reputations may be. We can choose to repair any breaches of trust among old friends and build up new levels of trust among others. We must do that if we want to develop intimate friendships.

Intimacy involves vulnerability and the risk of allowing friends a glimpse at the inside of us. An old Arabian proverb confirms this: "A friend is one to whom one may pour out all the contents of one's heart, chaff and grain together, knowing that the gentlest of hands will take and sift it, keep what is worth keeping and with the breath of kindness blow the rest away."

Chapter 7

Pray With
Your Friends

Do you remember the old saying, "The family that prays together stays together"? I think the same principle applies to our other relationships as well. There's something about bathing a relationship in prayer that puts it on a different level than average relationships. Prayer transforms the average relationship into a deeper and more intimate one.

Perhaps this deepening occurs because prayer purifies our motives and strengthens our patience. Mark Twain observed in *Huckleberry Finn*, "You can't pray a lie—I found that out."[1] It's true. Praying with our friends, I believe, promotes honesty and integrity in a relationship, teaching us to trust one another more.

Praying together also emphasizes our dependence on one another. It is often difficult for Christians to admit to being dependent on others, but, like it or not, we have not advanced so far that we don't need each other. We especially need close friends during these troublesome times of increased violence, crime and fraud. I can think of at least five reasons we need to pray together as friends.

The first reason friends should pray together is to help each other overcome the wrongful plottings of enemies and opponents. (2 Cor. 1:8-11; 2 Thess. 3:1,2.) Not many of us experience the complex intrigues of political life with its backstabbing and betrayal. But on a more realistic level, we all must deal with fellow employees, competitors and social acquaintances who sometimes seem to undermine and discredit us.

The second reason friends should pray together is that prayer opens doors that might otherwise be closed. Prayer opens doors to proclaim the gospel of Jesus Christ. (Col. 4:3.) Doors that appear to be closed to employment, ministry, promotion and relationships can all be opened through prayer.

Many a Christian has had to pray through doors that Satan has closed against him or her from time to time. Well, corporate prayer can change all that. By praying together, believers can create in the spirit divine opportunities for success, which can be walked out in the natural.

The third reason we should pray with our friends is to help one another overcome spiritual attacks. (Eph. 6:12,18.) Because life moves along fairly routinely, we often forget that Satan launches spiritual attacks daily, and even hourly. For this reason, we must pray continually for spiritual power.

The fourth reason friends should pray together is to help one another overcome trying circumstances. Each of us experiences times of loneliness, frailty and discouragement. It's interesting that the serious crises usually do not fell a strong Christian. Usually it's the trifles of the day-to-day walk that chop away at his roots until he falls. But when we pray together, it helps us keep life in perspective and prevents these trying circumstances from overwhelming us.

The fifth reason friends should pray together is that praying together provides spiritual power. "No great spiritual awakening has begun anywhere in the world apart from united prayer—

Christians persistently praying for revival," says J. Edwin Orr in *Prayer, Its Deeper Dimensions.*[2]

One of the best scriptural examples of praying with friends is found in Acts 4:23-31. Peter and John had been taken before the Jerusalem council for claiming that Jesus had been raised from the dead and for healing a man who had been lame for forty years. As the council could not discredit Peter and John, they released them, charging them not to speak in the name of Jesus—a limitation Peter and John could not accept.

The first thing Peter and John did after being released was to go to their friends, who, sensing the seriousness of the situation, prayed with them. Very specifically, they prayed that God would change the situation—and He did. He empowered them with the Holy Spirit to preach God's message boldly.

Praying together is so vital to a relationship that we dare not ignore or omit it from our lives. However, we should not only pray together; we should pray for one another too.

In the poem *The Passing of Arthur,* Tennyson wrote:

If thou shouldst never see my face again,
Pray for my soul. More things are wrought by prayer
Than this world dreams of. Wherefore, let thy voice
Rise like a fountain for me night and day
For what are men better than sheep or goats
That nourish a blind life within the brain,
If, knowing God, they lift not hands or prayer
Both for themselves and those who call them friend?
For so the whole round earth is every way
Bound by gold chains about the feet of God.[3]

What a beautiful way to express the power of prayer that bonds friends together.

Chapter 8

Be There in Triumph and Tragedy

Unfortunately, tragedies, such as the death of a loved one, a severe illness or even a loss of income, can occur in our lives at any time. I know firsthand what this is like.

Tragedy first raised its ugly head against our family when Tammy, our daughter, was hit by an automobile, causing near-fatal injuries. We experienced another great tragedy when our son Jeffrey was killed at the age of fifteen while working in our church. In both instances, my wife, Sharon, and I felt shock, fear and grief.

Both times, our friends and family came to support us. They allowed us to talk—rehearsing over and over what we knew about the events. Little did they realize that by listening they were helping us face the tragedies and cope with the great loss of our son and the injuries our daughter suffered. Some of our family and friends quietly assumed practical tasks, staying in the background while serving us. Nevertheless, we were aware of their presence and grateful for their love. They may not have said much, but they certainly did help.

I must honestly say that not everything our friends said made sense to us at the time of our son's death, but we greatly appreciated their comforting words. Their presence spoke volumes about their love and support for us. We knew they had not experienced the same pain we were experiencing, so what they said came from their perception of the events and not their own personal experiences with that type of loss. But what our friends *said* did not matter as much as what they *did*. Their *being there* was the most important thing.

The day after our son was killed, our house was crowded with many friends and family members. The phone rang continually. One of the calls came from a close friend who was offering sympathy, but I wasn't up to talking then. So I told the person who answered the phone to tell him I didn't feel like talking at the moment and to call back a little later. I knew he would understand because he was a close friend.

Time went on, but he didn't call me back nor did he attend the funeral. A few days went by, and I called him. I quickly found him to be very cold. Obviously, something was bothering him. As I began to question him about what was wrong, he said, "I was hurt because you didn't take my phone call, and I decided I was not as important to you as those well-known ministers whose calls you did take."

What he didn't know was that I hadn't taken many calls from well-known ministers. Furthermore, this friend could not have known that the way my son had been killed had devastated me. Otherwise, he would not have acted so selfishly.

I was hurt deeply by this friend's selfishness. If he had called because he truly loved me, he wouldn't have cared that he didn't get through right away. Instead of understanding that I was in great pain and asking what he could do to help, he expected more from me than I could give. He allowed the devil to talk him into a state of offense. And because of his offense, I never could restore this relationship to its former state, though I did all I knew to do.

Conversely, during that time of tragedy, we formed a deep relationship with one acquaintance whom we hadn't known very well before our son's death. But this person made it a point to be there for us. By the time he called I had regained some control and was able to talk on the phone. He was filled with compassion for us and said, "My wife and I are coming to be with you and Sharon. We just want to love you and minister to you."

They hardly knew us! In fact, a week before he came to us he had been given a great opportunity to speak at a convention.

"Thank you for your concern for us," I told him, " but I believe you should go on to your speaking engagement."

He kept insisting that he come to visit us, but I convinced him that many people were loving and ministering to us already. With those assurances, he went on to the convention, but he called regularly. And afterward he and his wife did come to see us. He even invited me to speak at his church, and a great relationship developed. Today he is one of my closest friends, largely because he and his wife unselfishly loved and cared for us.

We should desire to be with our friends and family during times of pain, grief or shock—without making demands on them or seeking our own interests. We need to become sensitive to our friends' needs, realizing that the things that don't seem particularly overwhelming to us may be devastating tragedies to them.

As I mentioned before, Jeffrey's death devastated Sharon and me. People who had never lost a son or daughter or anyone close in their lives told us how we should and could come through this. Their advice was good because it came from the Word. And we tried to live by the Word as much as possible without letting our emotions overwhelm us, but we were hurting. Oh, how we were hurting.

Now, because of their own beliefs, some of the people who tried to help us would not let us admit to them how much we were suffering—even though such an admission would have been therapeutic for us. My wife and I made it through by the Word and by our trust in God. But some of the same people who told us not to admit we were hurting were devastated and overcome themselves when a similar tragedy occurred in their own lives.

One couple even had to stop ministering because of their grief. But we didn't look at them and say, "Yes, it's different now that the experience is happening to you, isn't it?" No, we ran to them with compassion and understanding because we knew what they were experiencing.

Just a few weeks after our son was killed, I went to a convention, even though I was hurting badly inside. I loved and respected the minister who was speaking, and his message was great and very helpful. But right near the end of his sermon, he looked in my direction and said, "This will keep your kids from getting killed."

Needless to say, I was shocked for a few minutes. But after a while I got myself together. He was preaching under the anointing and was not thinking of what had happened to me. Of course, he would never intentionally have hurt me, so I decided to overlook it and go on.

You see, we need godly relationships that are not built on feelings but on love. When we build our relationships on love, it prevents us from misinterpreting the actions of our friends. Love is a decision, not a feeling. Love will cause us to stand by our friends as much as possible during times of tragedy.

Chapter 9

Allow Your Friends To Grow

As a relationship progresses, it should grow stronger and become richer as both people work on it together. But what sometimes happens is that the relationship falters because the people involved drift apart rather than becoming closer. Often, one party may begin to withdraw emotionally from the other. One may grow and develop spiritually, emotionally or even intellectually, whereas the other may not.

Each of us grows in different ways and at different times. The important thing to remember is that if we are to have strong relationships with others, we need to accept others in their particular stages of personal growth and development.

One of the biggest deterrents to personal growth is what I call "emotional blackmail." Emotional blackmail occurs when one person in the relationship manipulates the other person, which prevents him from growing or causes him to hang back emotionally. This practice is simply not reasonable and should not be used among individuals who are knit together by God. Each of us is gifted and talented in various areas, and these gifts should be used to enrich, and not abuse, one another.

We cannot control what people do to us, but we can control how we respond to them. Therefore, we must guard our hearts. If we constantly give license to our emotions, we can expect our relationships with others to become extremely fragile. Likewise, if we continually lose our tempers or respond irrationally to others, people will eventually begin to avoid us. However, if we deal with others from hearts of love, others will be attracted to us.

Reacting emotionally can be as simple as not thinking before we respond. Proverbs 18:13 says, **He that answereth a matter before he heareth it, it is folly and shame unto him.** Moreover, Proverbs 23:9 NIV warns, **Do not speak to a fool, for he will scorn the wisdom of your words.**

Obviously, God wants us to think a matter through before responding. It is better for us to keep silent and consider what we might say first than to speak rashly. We should think about how Jesus might respond and model our actions after His example.

Some people react emotionally by pulling back from relationships when they don't get their own way. Others talk out of both sides of their mouths, saying, "Accept me as I am, but *you* have to be what *I* want you to be." Harboring either of these attitudes forms no basis for a lasting relationship. Instead, it creates a double standard and undermines trust.

I believe relationships should be able to last through problems and difficult times; however, there will be no foundation on which to stand if we attempt to control one another.

Some people react emotionally in relationships, thereby preventing others from being themselves. Of course, both parties won't always agree on everything; but we can release one another to be individuals, thereby setting each other free.

Remember to give people room to grow and develop. As people grow individually, they can pour back a rich variety of experience, knowledge and wisdom into their relationships, which will benefit everyone involved.

Chapter 10

Demand Nothing in Return

No friend, no matter how close or compatible, will ever respond in exactly the same way we would respond in any given situation. Often, we forget that our friends are different from us. We forget that they may view life from a different perspective. And usually our friends have different backgrounds, goals, priorities and emotional responses than we do. This may sound basic, but it's true. These differences are what make a friendship rich and diverse.

It would be nice if we could always get along with our friends, with our personalities dovetailing together perfectly. But life doesn't always work that way. There will be times when each of us will have to stand alone. We may even become angry because our friends can't always meet our needs. We may also feel hurt because they don't do things for us in exactly the same way we would do things for them.

When this happens, we must remember that our friends can give only from what they have. Our best course of action is to expect nothing and to receive each response as though it were a gift to be enjoyed and treasured. For truly it is, especially if it is the person's best.

Sometimes, however, it's difficult to remember this principle when our perception differs from our friend's perception.

So much of what we see depends on where we're standing when we look. It's quite possible that our friends are seeing something altogether different than we are. Consequently, they may prescribe a different solution to a problem than we would. And although it may seem right to them, that solution may not work in our situations.

Additionally, our friends don't always know how we'll receive the advice they give. That's because our friends' perceptions are based on what they see and not always on what we see.

It helps to remember that the very qualities that draw us to individuals usually have a flip side that can also repel us. For example, one may be drawn by another's sensitive and tender nature, but repelled by his indecisiveness and passivity. Or one may admire a friend's assertiveness, but become appalled at how difficult it is for him to relinquish control. This demonstrates that we cannot expect all of our needs to be met by any one friend. As we have limitations on receiving, our friends also have limitations on giving. Conversely, we may have limitations on our giving, and our friends may have limitations on their receiving.

You see, no one person can possibly satisfy all of our needs. That's why it's important to accept the limitations of our friends. Receive each moment of friendship as a gift and hold it close. If we collect such moments from many friends, we will live full, rich lives.

Chapter 11

Show Gratitude

If we are to maintain healthy friendships with others, it's vital that we show gratitude. Accepting what friends have to give without expecting more in return frees us from becoming let down. However, giving to others out of love and a desire to help and demanding nothing in return does *not* free us from our responsibility to show gratitude toward both God and others. Others may not always show you gratitude for the things you have done for them, but even if they don't, you are to continue to walk in love toward them. Remember, if they don't do what they should, you are still to do what is right.

Jesus was very clear in His teaching on this subject.

As He was going into a village one day, ten men who had leprosy met Him. There they stood at a distance and called out in a loud voice, **Jesus, Master, have pity on us!** (Luke 17:13).

When He saw them, He said, **Go, shew yourselves unto the priests** (v. 14). And as they went, they were cleansed.

One of them, a Samaritan, when he saw that he was healed, went back, praising God in a loud voice. He threw himself at Jesus' feet, thanking Him for what He had done. (vv. 15,16.)

Jesus then asked the Samaritan, "Were not all ten cleansed? Where are the other nine? Was no one found to return and give praise to God except this foreigner?" (vv. 17,18.)

Then He said to him, "Rise and go; your faith has made you well." (v. 19.)

Immediately before Jesus told this story, He asked His disciples whether a master owed thanks to a servant who had simply done his duty. In both of these examples, Jesus used two Greek words to paint a picture of the importance of gratitude. The two Greek words He used were *charis* and *eucharisteo*. The first word *charis* is commonly translated "grace" and carries three major meanings, namely, (1) that which bestows pleasure, delight or favorable regard; (2) that which proceeds from a friendly disposition and manifests in acts of kindness, such as graciousness, lovingkindness, goodwill and gratitude; (3) the spiritual state of those who have experienced that part of God's character that dispenses mercy and favor.[1]

The first meaning of the Greek word *charis* is usually applied to the beauty and gracefulness of a person, those qualities that draw us to another. The second meaning stresses the freedom and spontaneity of these attitudes as contrasted to debt or obligation. We can clearly see this meaning of the word as demonstrated by God's redemptive mercy and His gracious plans to bless those who are obedient to His Word. Additionally, we see it demonstrated when Jesus said others would know we were His disciples because we loved one another. (John 13:35.)

The third meaning of the word *charis* is the one we hear most often. It denotes the quality of life one possesses after his sins are forgiven and he has gained God's mercy and favor.

The second Greek word Jesus uses in this passage is *eucharisteo,* which is akin to the word *charis,* denoting gratitude and thankfulness. *"Thanksgiving* is the expression of joy Godward," wrote W.E. Vine, "and is therefore the fruit of the Spirit" (Gal. 5:22); "believers are encouraged to abound in it" (e.g., Col. 2:7; Col. 3:15).[2]

> But when the Holy Spirit controls our lives he will produce this kind of fruit in us: love, *joy,* peace, patience, kindness, goodness, faithfulness, gentleness and self-control; and here there is no conflict with the Jewish laws.
>
> Galatians 5:22 TLB

> Let your roots grow down into him and draw up nourishment from him. See that you go on growing in the Lord, and become strong and vigorous in the truth you were taught. Let your lives overflow with *joy and thanksgiving* for all he has done.
>
> Colossians 2:7 TLB

> Let the peace of heart which comes from Christ be always present in your hearts and lives, for this is your responsibility and privilege as members of his body. *And always be thankful.*
>
> Colossians 3:15 TLB

It is obvious from these Scriptures that we have a responsibility to be grateful to others. Additionally, if we are to be like Christ, we are to cultivate a spirit of gratitude. If it is important to show gratitude to God for His providence and blessings, then it is also important to thank those who perform acts of kindness or give us gifts.

Beyond the usual expressions of gratitude—written and verbal—there is another way of showing gratitude that comes from an outgrowth of one's character. It describes a way of life. It, too, is a manifestation of the second meaning of the word *charis,* that which proceeds from a friendly disposition and manifests in acts of kindness, such as graciousness, loving-kindness, goodwill and gratitude.

The word *goodwill* implies both a cheerful willingness to do something and the favor that one has acquired beyond the mere value of what one sells. Though used most often in the business sense, the word is appropriately applied to individuals and the agreements we make. The way in which we handle our agreements, whether interpersonal or in business, expresses our gratitude for the efforts of others and the opportunities we have.

Jesus gave us some important guidelines to follow, which are found in Matthew 20:

> **For the Kingdom of Heaven is like the owner of an estate who went out early one morning to hire workers for his vineyard. He agreed to pay the normal daily wage and sent them out to work.**
>
> **At nine o'clock in the morning he was passing through the marketplace and saw some people standing around doing nothing. So he hired them, telling them he would pay them whatever was right at the end of the day.**
>
> **At noon and again around three o'clock he did the same thing.**

At five o'clock that evening he was in town again and saw some more people standing around. He asked them, "Why haven't you been working today?"

They replied, "Because no one hired us." The owner of the estate told them, "Then go on out and join the others in my vineyard."

That evening he told the foreman to call the workers in and pay them, beginning with the last workers first. When those hired at five o'clock were paid, each received a full day's wage. When those hired earlier came to get their pay, they assumed they would receive more. But they too, were paid a day's wage. When they received their pay, they protested, "Those people worked only one hour, and yet you've paid them just as much as you paid us who worked all day in the scorching heat."

He answered one of them, "Friend, I haven't been unfair! Didn't you agree to work all day for the usual wage? Take it and go. I wanted to pay this last worker the same as you. Is it against the law for me to do what I want with my money? Should you be angry because I am kind?"

And so it is that many who are first now will be last then; and those who are last now will be first then.

Matthew 20:1-16 NLT

Here, Jesus stresses the importance of keeping our agreements. Whether favorable or not, once we give our word, we should demonstrate gratitude by being bound to it. Sadly, all of us can tell stories about making agreements that were not in our best interests. The principle Jesus was talking about, however, is that we should do what we agreed to do.

When we accept a responsibility to do something, we should live up to it. From time to time, people complain about how they aren't being treated fairly in the workplace. This may be true, but if the terms of the contract or agreement are being met, they need to remember that they agreed to fulfill those terms.

Whenever we find ourselves in negotiations with a prospective employer, for example, we should ask questions until we understand all that is expected of us. Doing so can prevent future misunderstandings and broken obligations.

Money is often a source of misunderstanding during such negotiations. For example, some feel they are not paid enough, while others feel they are overpaid. If someone discovers, for instance, that he is doing essentially the same job as someone else but making less money, he is likely to complain and begin to sow discord, compounding the problem.

Sowing discord is wrong, and should be avoided.

> **For there are six things the Lord hates—no, seven: Haughtiness, lying, murdering, plotting evil, eagerness to do wrong, a false witness and *sowing discord among brothers.***
>
> **Proverbs 6:16-19 TLB**

God's principles never change. As long as we're not suffering abuse or harm, we need to fulfill the agreements we've made with others. Whatever we do should be done as unto God, faithfully and loyally, without allowing wrong attitudes to control us. When we fulfill our obligations with right attitudes, we ensure God's blessings on us.

And whatever you do or say, let it be as a representative of the Lord Jesus, and come with him into the presence of God the Father to give him your thanks.

You slaves must always obey your earthly masters, not only trying to please them when they are watching you but all the time; obey them willingly because of your love for the Lord and because you want to please him. Work hard and cheerfully at all you do, just as though you were working for the Lord and not merely for your masters, remembering that it is the Lord Christ who is going to pay you, giving you your full portion of all he owns. He is the one you are really working for. And if you don't do your best for him, he will pay you in a way that you won't like—for he has no special favorites who can get away with shirking.

Colossians 3:17,22-25 TLB

Expressing gratitude includes keeping your word, being careful about punctuality, keeping rules and not bending them, respecting others' property and time and honoring the skills and talents of the person with whom you made the agreement. This does not mean, however, that you must continue working with someone after the end of an agreement. You have the right to seek other employment or to renegotiate new agreements. The important thing is to remember to keep the right attitude, because everything you do reveals your character. And your character is supposed to mirror Jesus.

PART II

Fix Yourself First

Chapter 12

Know Who You Are

When my wife discovered who she was in Christ, it changed her life. When she found out her rights and privileges in Christ, she went from a state of insecurity to confidence, from being reticent to being a conversationalist, from being a follower to being a leader. Perhaps some of the secrets she learned will help you too. I've listed below some of the revelations she discovered.

Self-Worth Comes From Christ

As Christians, we should know that our value comes from Jesus Christ. In Christ, we become all that God requires of us, all that it was impossible for us to become in ourselves. This right standing with God isn't earned through obedience to any law or through any means other than faith in Jesus Christ.

Faith Comes From Christ

As Christians, our faith is in Jesus Christ. And that faith is always based on the relationship we have with God through the knowledge we have of Him from His Word. Faith is not a force that we control and use to manipulate God; instead, it is the recognition that God is faithful to Himself and to His promises. We know we can trust God to fulfill His Word.

Goodness Comes From Christ

Our goodness comes from being in Jesus Christ. The Bible says there is none good but one, and that is Jesus. (Rom. 3:10-12.) Even with our best efforts, we fail to measure up to the requirements of God's Word. We need not expect that we become good by obeying, because none of us can obey perfectly every command. It is, therefore, necessary that we believe our goodness lies in faith in Jesus Christ.

Spiritual Knowledge Comes From Christ

The basis for our spiritual knowledge comes from Jesus Christ. The more we learn, the more we realize how much we don't know. As we anchor ourselves in the knowledge of Jesus Christ and God's Word, most things fall into place. This perspective gives us the freedom to explore additional information without fear of losing our faith. Then, as information is judged by using God's Word as a guide, we can either accept it or reject it, accordingly.

Self-Control Comes From Christ

The ability to control our fleshly appetites is reinforced when we base our lives in Jesus Christ and His Word. It is only when we allow Jesus to control our lives that we can learn to say no to fleshly impulses that could destroy our lives and the lives of loved ones. Only then are we strong enough to trust God and think of the consequences our actions can have, rather than to act on impulses.

Let's look at a familiar Bible story to illustrate this principle. When King Saul began to persecute David, David could have taken Saul's life many times and become king of Israel. But David restrained himself because he understood that not all opportunities are just. Authority is entrusted by God, and it should not be abused.

Perseverance Comes From Christ

As Christians, we have the ability to persevere during adversity because of who we are in Jesus Christ. Jesus gives us the ability to remain steadfast and to persevere in the face of hardships and adversities. He gives us the ability to accomplish His work in the face of ridicule or public disapproval. With Christ, we can be victorious.

Holiness Comes From Christ

By studying the life of Jesus, we are taught to fear and reverence God by seeking to please Him. That, I think, is what holiness is all about. Too often, we excuse ourselves from genuinely pleasing God and rationalize our actions because we see others who are talking and acting differently. But I believe God is looking for people who want to walk uprightly before Him more than anything else in life.

Kindness Comes From Christ

When Jesus abides within us, we have the desire to perform acts of kindness for people—beginning with members of our own families and extending outward to complete strangers. Class distinctions disappear when we truly try to live our lives based on the example of Jesus Christ.

Love Comes From Christ

The ability to love one another with an agape love is found when we live our lives in Jesus Christ. He enables us to willingly forget ourselves and to devote and commit our lives to serving God first and then others. He is the One who gives us agape love—that perfect, nonjudgmental love that caused Him to give His life for us.

When we know who we are in Christ, we should stop looking for reasons to find fault or to blame others. But if we find that we have done that, we need to say, "I'm sorry; I was wrong."

Chapter 13

Find Out Who You Truly Are and Be That Person

How can we be true to ourselves if we don't know who we are and don't have any idea how to find out? We can't. We know we're supposed to be "real," but what does that mean? In the children's classic, *The Velveteen Rabbit*, Margery Williams describes being real as being loved. Although on the surface the story is about toys which become real, this allegory teaches children how they can become genuine, or real. The book goes on to explain that one can be loved only when one becomes him- or herself, complete with faults and strengths, but without pretense or artifice.[1]

According to the story, the velveteen rabbit felt insignificant and quite commonplace because he was not expensive or mechanical. He had no moving parts, modern ideas or pretense. He could not refer to his technical makeup because he was stuffed only with sawdust, which was quite out-of-date.

The velveteen rabbit's only friend was another toy, which was called the Skin Horse. The Skin Horse had lived longer in the nursery than any of the others. He was so old that his brown coat was bald in patches and his seams showed. Most of the hair in his tail had been pulled out and used as string for bead necklaces. Although he was unsightly, he was wise, for he had seen a long succession of mechanical toys arrive and boast and swagger about, only later to see their mainsprings break.

The Skin Horse knew they were only toys, and he knew they would never turn into anything else. "Nursery magic" is very strange and wonderful, but only those playthings that are old, wise and experienced, like the Skin Horse, understand this.

"What is REAL?" asked the Rabbit one day, when they were lying side by side near the nursery fender, before Nana came to tidy the room. "Does it mean having things that buzz inside you and a stick-out handle?"

"Real isn't how you are made," said the Skin Horse. "It's a thing that happens to you. When a child loves you for a long, long time, not just to play with, but really loves you, then you become real."

"Does it hurt?" asked the Rabbit.

"Sometimes," said the Skin Horse, for he was always truthful. "When you are real, you don't mind being hurt."

"Does it happen all at once, like being wound up," he asked, "or bit by bit?"

"It doesn't happen all at once," said the Skin Horse. "You become. It takes a long time. That's why it doesn't often happen to people who break easily, or have sharp edges, or who have to be carefully kept. Generally, by the time you are real, most of your hair has been loved off, and your eyes drop out and you get loose in the joints and very shabby. But these things don't matter at all, because once you are real, you can't be ugly, except to people who don't understand. ...but once you are real you can't become unreal again. It lasts for always."[2]

Margery Williams is telling children they shouldn't be proud or haughty, or pretend to be more than they are if they expect to be real. Neither should we.

The Scriptures remind us against being high-minded, haughty and proud. These attitudes cause us to be ashamed of our "sawdust" and prevent our acknowledging who we really are. Sometimes we hide for so long behind these attitudes that we need to rediscover who we are.

In his book *Making Friends (& Making Them Count)*, E.M. Griffin suggests a simple way of discovering who we are. He said we should find a quiet place and spend five to seven minutes making a list of fifteen or more responses to the question, *Who am I?*[3]

After we've finished, we should look over the list and separate the nouns from the adjectives. Generally, the nouns will represent our identity, that "mind's-eye picture we have of ourselves." This picture, he says, helps us focus on who we are and see how we differ from everyone else. "If we know what to expect from ourselves, that's one less variable to worry about. We can concentrate on other people's actions and external circumstances. We don't have to stew over our own response."[4]

The adjectives on E.M. Griffin's list represent our self-esteem, how we feel about ourselves. Most of us will include both positive and negative adjectives on our lists. We should recognize that the adjectives we view as negative may not appear to someone else to be negatives. However, we should try to improve in the areas where we feel weak, rather than subjecting ourselves to harsh criticism and self-contempt.[5]

To feel good about ourselves, each of us needs strong self-esteem in four areas: a sense of moral worth, a sense of competence, a sense of self-determination and a sense of unity.

A Sense of Moral Worth

We need to know that we have been forgiven, that we are living according to God's will. This sense of moral worth prevents feelings of self-condemnation, guilt and fear, all of which can quickly undermine any relationship.

A Sense of Competence

We all need to know that we can do something well; no one can do everything well, but we can all do something well. Even if our competence is strong in only one area, it will give us a sense of fulfillment, achievement and intrinsic worth. This feeling of competence is tied to our expectations. Low expectations and poor performance equal a sense of incompetence. If our expectations are unrealistically high and our skill levels are low, our sense of competence will drop. But if, on the other hand, our skills match our expectations, our sense of competence will be strong.

A Sense of Self-Determination

A strong sense of self-determination will allow us the freedom to make our own decisions and our own choices. So with a strong sense of self-determination, we will be better able to direct the course of our lives.

A Sense of Unity

We should never feel as though there's a part of us that is incongruent (in disagreement) with any other part. All parts of our nature should dovetail to make a whole person. For example, if we love being with people, we should enjoy people in every aspect of life.[6] A strong sense of unity helps us feel whole.

A good sense of moral worth, competence, self-determination and unity are the building blocks of our own personalities, and, consequently, the building blocks of our relationships. When we know ourselves and are true to our ideals, it is easier for us to build relationships with others.

Shakespeare illustrated this principle, albeit more dramatically, in Hamlet: "This above all: to thine own self be true, and it must follow, as the night the day, thou canst not then be false to any man."[7]

Chapter 14

Live Close
to God in
Your Heart

The key to finding out who we are is to find out who God is. Develop a close relationship with God first, and all other relationships will fall into place. Jesus' first and last words to His disciples were, and still are, "Follow Me!"

How then do we live close to Christ? How do we follow Him? Oswald J. Smith gives us a clue in his book *The Man God Uses.* He says there are three supreme tests to determine whether we are living close to God in our hearts: the supreme tests of discipleship, conduct and service.[1]

According to Smith, living close to God in our hearts involves passing the first supreme test of discipleship. The outline for this test can be seen in the Bible passage in which Jesus, after His crucifixion, prepared to go and be with the Father.

Jesus went to His disciples early one morning after they had fished all night but caught nothing. On that occasion, Jesus asked Peter the ultimate question about discipleship. He asked Peter if he loved Him.

Notice that Jesus did not seem to be interested in Peter's doctrine or dogma; He didn't ask whether Peter had memorized all the creeds or if his theology was totally accurate. He simply asked: "Peter, do you love Me?"

Furthermore, Jesus didn't inquire as to whether Peter had confessed and repented of all of his sins. He didn't seem to be interested in what services Peter had performed for the church either. He simply asked, "Peter, do you love Me?"

You see, we can be active church members who know every nuance of doctrine and can even repeat all the creeds—and we can do it all without loving God in our hearts. It is even possible to be a martyr and yet not love God. But we *cannot* be His disciples unless we love Him more than anything else. Loving God is a key to living close to Him in our hearts.

According to Smith, the second test to living close to God in our hearts is the supreme test of conduct. Although it may be hard to imagine, we can get to the point where we love God so much we will no longer need to question our conduct before Him. Questions such as "Is this wrong?" or "May I do this or that?" are decided on the basis of our great love for God.

We can actually get to the point where our great love for God can so permeate our hearts that there will be no room for sin, no room for the world and no desire for things that delight the unsaved. Our sole desire can be to please Him in all things, at all times.

Smith's third test to living a life close to God in our hearts is the supreme test of service. One who truly loves God serves Him because he loves Him, not because he feels a sense of duty or obligation. His service in itself brings him unspeakable joy and peace. The true servant of God is willing to lay down his life for God if need be. Proof of this is found throughout the annals of history in the lives of the following people who laid down their lives for God: Stephen, the first martyr; Peter and the early apostles; Paul; Brainerd, Judson, Livingstone, Morrison, Taylor,

Carey and all the great missionaries of the past; Charles Spurgeon, Billy Sunday, Dwight L. Moody, Praying Hyde, William Gurnall, Watchman Nee, and an endless list of disciples who truly loved God.

In his sermon titled "The Bride," J. B. Stoney says:

> I know that I am united to Christ [when] I am so identified with His interests that they are paramount with me. The leading characteristic of union is that your individuality is merged in Christ. You belong entirely to another. The bride is merged in the Bridegroom.
>
> Then follows the effect of union.... The first is, "That Christ may dwell in your heart by faith...." Next, you are brought to scan the range of His glory, to "comprehend with all saints what is the breadth, and length, and depth, and height." And lastly, to crown all, to "know the love of Christ which passeth knowledge."[2]

So, how do we live close to God in our hearts? How do we follow Christ wholeheartedly? By loving Him above all others. Then, after we love Him, we can love others.

Chapter 15

Avoid Seeking the Approval of Others

Lester Sumrall, a great missionary evangelist of the mid-twentieth century, said, "I never seek the applause of people and I'm never moved by their criticism." The biographies of many of the church's greatest men and women reveal that these people always sought God's approval over man's. Peter and a group of disciples were commanded by the Jewish council in Jerusalem not to teach in the name of Jesus, but Peter replied, **We ought to obey God rather than men** (Acts 5:29).

Sadly, not everyone seeks God's approval first; many go to extraordinary lengths to attain man's approval. This generally indicates insecurity and a lack of self-confidence. Some people even *surround* themselves with people who applaud them, say how great they are and tell them only what they want to hear. These types of people may preach great sermons, write great books or sing beautifully, but they are typically unable to handle ordinary interactions with people, except when receiving praise from them. I believe we should not give groundless approbation to such individuals, because it is spiritually detrimental to them.

We would have no need to seek man's approval if we would follow God's instructions and allow the teaching of His Word to change our hearts. It is important to realize that we already have the approval of God.

As I search the Scriptures, over and over I find encouragement to seek God's approval. In fact, one of the Greek words the Bible uses to describe this kind of approval is *dokimazo;* its adjectival derivative is *dokimos.* Both are used primarily to describe metals and invariably mean "to test with the expectation of approving." The word was first used in Genesis 23:16 regarding 400 shekels of silver being approved. In 1 Thessalonians 2:4, Paul and his fellow missionaries were "approved of God to be entrusted with the Gospel." This did not mean they were given permission to preach; rather, *they received divine approval after they had been divinely tested.*

Paul urged young Timothy, **Study to shew thyself approved unto God, a workman that needeth not to be ashamed, rightly dividing the word of truth** (2 Tim. 2:15). In other words, Timothy was to seek to meet God's test with the expectation of winning God's approval. So it should be with us. If we seek God's will and approval first, we will never have cause to fear any man. This is especially important to remember in relationships where peer pressure is greater than our own common sense. If we would truly seek God regarding every aspect of each relationship, we would not be insecure or envious of others.

Chapter 16

Get Into the Relationship for the Right Reason

Relationships that last are built on love and trust. That's why it is important for us to examine our motives for establishing each relationship. We should ask ourselves, *Why am I seeking to be involved with this individual?*

Are we seeking prestige through association? This often happens when we try to position ourselves to form relationships with those who have achieved success in their fields, such as successful pastors, business executives, political leaders or celebrities. There is certainly nothing wrong with offering friendship to these people; but if we are trying to use friendship merely to achieve status for ourselves, then we need to examine our motives.

Are we seeking someone to lean on? Sometimes we form relationships of codependency, which lead to disastrous results and suffering. We should work to feel confident within ourselves and to give constructively to our relationships, rather than constantly taking from them. In *Seeds of Greatness,* Denis Waitley says, "We must feel love inside ourselves before we can give it to others."[1]

Perhaps we are seeking relationships simply as an attempt to position ourselves for social or business introductions. A more honest approach would be to introduce ourselves directly to the individuals whom we seek to contact.

A mature relationship is many-faceted, involves the total person—physical, social, intellectual and spiritual aspects—and must focus on interaction with the other person through love and trust. Immature relationships focus on only one or two areas of an individual and quickly falter when other areas are displayed.[2] If we cannot respect the total person, how can we love and trust the person?

"With love, there can be no fear," Waitley continues. "Love is natural and unconditional. Love asks no questions—neither preaching nor demanding; neither comparing nor measuring. Love is pure and simple—the greatest value of all."[3]

What are we looking for in any given relationship? The answer to this question will determine whether we should proceed with it. Once we've answered that question, we need to make sure we proceed in the relationship for the right reasons.

Chapter 17

Before we get involved in any relationship, we should ask ourselves why we want to be involved with this particular individual or group of individuals. We could save ourselves a lot of potential hurt if we would learn to judge our own motivations first.

We should never get into a relationship because of our own feelings of rejection or insecurity. Signals of feelings of rejection include such things as making a big deal out of someone's failing to speak to us in a group setting. Remember, our feelings can sometimes mislead us. Perhaps people who seem to ignore us simply do not see us, have something else on their minds or are in a hurry. We don't always know what is going on in another person's life at any given moment.

We exhibit signals of insecurity when we believe someone is talking about us. This usually happens when a person in a group looks in our direction and then begins to talk to someone. If we are insecure with ourselves, we might imagine that the person who is talking is saying all sorts of things about us. Big deal! No matter what he may say, it cannot change who we are. We decide that for ourselves by our choices, our actions and our motivations. When we look within and measure ourselves by the Word of God, we learn who we truly are. Besides, we can't control what other people say about us. So why worry?

If we are to build lasting relationships, we must rid ourselves of deep-seated feelings of rejection and insecurity. We do this by building ourselves up from the Word of God, acknowledging who we are in Jesus Christ and patterning our lives after the Master's life. And we know if we do this, we will excel in many things.

By doing this, we can give our attention to developing certain qualities within ourselves that will ensure long- lasting relationships. There are five qualities that I want to mention which will ensure that we build lasting relationships. They are selflessness, forbearance, attention, achievement and carefulness.

Selflessness

We must choose to have complete regard and consideration for the other party in every aspect of a relationship. No longer can we concentrate on ourselves only—on what pleases us—what we want to do, where we want to go and how we feel. This selfishness leads to failure and a breakdown in a relationship very quickly.

Forbearance

Sometimes our lives are filled with challenges and obstacles that need to be overcome. During these times, we will need friends to support us emotionally and to exercise forbearance with us. But the forbearance we get from our friends must be equally balanced; for example, we must not expect our friends to forbear with us through that which we are not willing to forbear with them. The virtue of forbearance is a two-way street.

Attention

Individuals involved in a relationship need to show each other some attention on a regular basis. That doesn't mean we need to shower inordinate or constant attention on our friends, but we do need to show them courtesy. We need to take the time to appreciate our friends. We must never take our friends for granted.

Achievement

We do not arrive at mature relationships overnight. We must develop them carefully over the years, giving special attention to those things that nurture and cultivate the relationship. Be patient with your friends, and allow the test of time to develop and strengthen your relationship. Only with this care can a relationship grow and develop properly.

Carefulness

Misunderstanding can occur easily and quickly if you let it. That's why it is so important to give the utmost care to a relationship, especially in places where a breakdown or lack of harmony in the friendship could occur. Whatever crises we may face in our lives, it is important to take time for our friends. It doesn't matter whether we receive comfort from them, give comfort to them, talk about an unusual situation or simply have a casual conversation.

As we continue to build lasting relationships with our friends, our motivation should be to incorporate these five qualities into our lives. As we do, we will find ourselves not only enjoying more satisfying friendships but growing toward greater maturity.

Chapter 18

Build Up
the Altar, Not
the Problem

Every relationship goes through rocky periods from time to time. I've discovered, however, that when we build our relationships around the altar of biblical principles instead of around the problems, we can overcome almost any obstacle. The more time we spend in the realm of the Holy Spirit rather than in the realm of our emotions, the more we will see problems objectively from a godly viewpoint.

As a youth in the beginning of my ministry, I was inexperienced and immature, but I wanted to make a difference for the kingdom of God. I would pour myself into teaching and training people only to find that those same people took what I had taught them and then abandoned me.

This hurt me, and I reacted emotionally and allowed some of my relationships to be broken. I withdrew from friends, using the excuse, "They hurt me; let them come to me to get this offense straightened out." Well, that's not the principle Jesus taught. He said, **Therefore, if you are offering your gift at the altar and there remember that your brother has something against you, leave your gift there in front of the altar. First go and be reconciled to your brother; then come and offer your gift** (Matt. 5:23,24 NIV).

I didn't want to accept this teaching, because I was hurting and responding emotionally to the pain. I had poured myself into these people, and they had responded by leaving my church and starting another church down the street. What they were doing was unethical, and I knew it.

Now, I could have prevented some of my pain had I released these people in my heart and let them go. But I thought, *It's not time for them to go, and the way they are doing this is not right. They are taking members out of this congregation, people whom we love and who love us. What they are doing is not right!*

That may have been true, but it was not my responsibility to change them. I was trying to hold on to something I had no control over. I reacted wrongly, and I did some wrong things because of what had been done to me. I justified my actions by thinking, *I'm the pastor here, and I'm trying to protect the people.*

In retrospect, I should have let those people go and ceased entertaining the daily feelings of hurt. I didn't guard my emotions; instead, I let them rule me. I should have taken this hurt to the altar and allowed the Spirit of God to let love flow through me, washing away the hurt so I could be restored.

Because of this offense and because I was trying to take responsibility for the actions of others, my relationship with these people was broken. Furthermore, it led to the breaking off of relationships with others who decided to leave my church and attend their churches.

During this whole episode God was talking to me, but I didn't listen. He would say again and again, *Take care of yourself, Don. Walk in love, Don. Do what you know is right. Treat people right. Treat these individuals right.* Somewhere along the way God finally got through to me, and I listened. I reached a point of maturity and realized I didn't have to respond emotionally. I found that I had to walk in the Spirit of God. And the only way I could do that was by overriding my emotions and preventing pride from ruling me. In time, thanks to God, this offense has been forgiven and the relationships have been restored.

I learned two major lessons from this incident. The first was to build around the altar, not the problem. In other words, I learned to take my problems to God and leave them with Him instead of carrying them myself. The second lesson I learned was that I don't have a right to control other people's actions.

I wish I had learned these lessons before the rupture in these relationships, but I'm grateful God was persistent in teaching me, regardless of my ignorance. I am also grateful to now walk in agreement with those same people who hurt me long ago.

PART III

Communicate, Communicate, Communicate

Chapter 19

Discuss Any Offenses With Your Friends Early and as Often as Needed

Offenses come to us all. We can't avoid them, but we can control how we respond to them. Let's look in the books of Matthew and Mark to see how Jesus taught us to handle them.

Therefore if thou bring thy gift to the altar, and there rememberest that thy brother hath aught against thee; leave there thy gift before the altar, and go thy way; first be reconciled to thy brother, and then come and offer thy gift.

Agree with thine adversary quickly, whiles thou art in the way with him; lest at any time the adversary deliver thee to the judge, and the judge deliver thee to the officer, and thou be cast into prison.

Verily I say unto thee, Thou shalt by no means come out thence, till thou hast paid the uttermost farthing.

Matthew 5:23-26

Now let's look at the same principle in Mark's gospel.

> And when ye stand praying, forgive, if ye have
> aught against any: that your Father also which is in
> heaven may forgive you your trespasses. But if ye do
> not forgive, neither will your Father which is in heaven
> forgive your trespasses.
>
> **Mark 11:25,26**

Notice the four steps Jesus outlined for the resolution of an offense: (1) Talk to the person who has something against you; (2) be reconciled with the person who has something against you; (3) agree or come to terms quickly; (4) forgive.

Talk to the Person
Who Has Something Against You

When someone takes offense at something you do or say, go and talk with that person. Find out what went wrong. Apparently, Jesus thought talking with an offended friend was more important than praying for him. At least He made it clear that the talking should be taken care of first, then the praying.

Jesus said we should go and talk about the offense as soon as we remember it. Now, this kind of talking implies a mutual discussion of what caused the offense, whereby each person hears and understands the other's position. It does not mean we should insist that we're right or refuse to hear the other person's side.

When someone is offended, we should look first to see if the problem is with us. The Bible speaks very plainly about this issue. If you have a plank in your own eye, how can you remove the splinter from your brother's? (Matt. 7:3-5.) If the problem is within us, we should deal with it first. We may not need to confront a friend, acquaintance or family member if we can see and admit to the problem within ourselves. If the problem does lie within us, we should repent and not blame someone else for the problem.

We should never go into a discussion with the attitude that we are trying to win. Avoid statements that claim someone is right or wrong. Rather, find the problem, solve it and move on.

Confrontation is not something I enjoy or look forward to, but as a leader I know it's sometimes part of my life. Most people will not confront other people about problems because of fear or a desire to avoid making matters worse. However, it is important to deal with problems as they occur.

We must not run, but we must deal with each situation according to the Scriptures.

As believers, we should be able to clear up misunderstandings and conflicts. This is not always easy. Sometimes when we confront individuals, even if we have the right spirit or attitude, they become even more offended. If that happens, and we have followed the steps Jesus outlined for resolving an offense, we should continue to treat them with love and not allow the devil to get us to take offense.

I would rather run the risk of losing a friendship by dealing with the problem than wonder what the problem was, simply because I didn't have the courage to confront the person.

This actually happened to me. I asked someone I thought I might have offended if anything was wrong, and he said, "Oh, no. I've just had problems of my own; that's why I've been distant." Well, I took this person at his word, and he is more distant now than he was before.

If someone is bothered by your asking an honest question, then you didn't have much of a friendship to begin with. Sometimes you have to let things go and move on. Trying to force a person to talk about something never works well.

Be Reconciled With the Person Who Caused the Offense

To reconcile with someone implies the giving and receiving of apologies. The Greek word *diallasso* "denotes mutual concession after mutual hostility."[1] Jesus said we should not complete our devotions until we are reconciled with our friends—and He is willing to wait for us to do so. That's heavy teaching, but I think Jesus was trying to stress the importance of our interpersonal relationships. Namely, that it's incumbent upon us to do the right thing regardless of the responses from others.

Get Into Agreement About Coming to Terms Quickly

Jesus taught that we should make reconciliation our top priority, seeking it without delay. The downfalls of not reconciling with our friends when possible can be great. For example, if we neglect reconciliation, not only may we lose friendships forever, but our friends may even take us to court. In the eyes of Jesus, this is a serious problem. He says our relationships affect our entire lives and, therefore, must be tended carefully. Perhaps He was thinking about the truth of Proverbs 18:19: *A brother offended is harder to be won than a strong city: and their contentions are like the bars of a castle.* Or, as *The Living Bible* says, **It is harder to win back the friendship of an offended brother than to capture a fortified city. His anger shuts you out like iron bars.**

Forgive

Forgive. There it is, the whole crux of the matter: Relationships are mended when we forgive. Jesus chose a word rich with meaning: *aphiemi*. This word technically means "to send away," but, in regard to debts, it denotes "complete cancellation." In other words, it means to cancel those debts forever. Or, in regard to sins, it denotes: "(a) the remission (release from or cancellation) of the punishment, (b) deliverance from the penalty, and (c) complete removal of the cause of offense."[2]

When we forgive in this manner, we cannot reinstate debts, punishments or penalties again. We are instructed to remove the cause of offense, however extreme that action may seem to us. Jesus illustrated this principle when He talked about cutting off the hand or foot, or plucking out the eye if it causes offense. (Matt. 18:7-9.) That's what Jesus did in the Atonement: He canceled our debts, punishments and penalties and removed the cause of our sins. All that remained was our acceptance of His forgiveness.

Jesus taught that we should forgive others as God forgives us—without limitation or conditions. He told Peter that he was obligated to forgive a person up to 490 times a day. (Matt. 18:21,22.) I believe the 490 times indicates not so much a specific number of times that we should forgive as much as it indicates our need to continually forgive one another. When we take this attitude, all that remains is for our friends to accept our forgiveness.

Sadly, some of our friends may choose not to accept our forgiveness when we've offended them. They may take themselves out of our lives and leave the relationship in the past.

This happened to Sharon and me during our early days in ministry. We had to start out small as we made the transition from an evangelistic focus to a pastoral focus. Our first congregation was small, and we usually went out to eat with several people after services. Eventually, we developed a close relationship with one couple in the church. In fact, we became the best of friends.

However, as the church began to grow, the pressures and responsibilities of a growing congregation caused the relationship to change. Sharon and I did not love the couple less. We just couldn't commit as much time to them as we had before.

Eventually, our best friends became offended and left the church. I tried to talk with them, but by that time it was too late. If I had explained to them early in the relationship that as the church grew we would have less time to spend with them, perhaps I could have prevented the offense. Although the relationship has since been restored, it has never been the same. As a result, I now try to communicate with my friends early and often about any potential difficulties.

Because God places such importance on our interpersonal relationships, it is vital that we talk with our friends about any offenses—early and often—always seeking reconciliation.

Chapter 20

Deal With Issues; Don't Run From Them

"Don't run *from* God when you do wrong; run *to* Him." What a powerful thought! The Scriptures teach, **If we confess our sins, he is faithful and just to forgive us our sins, and to cleanse us from all unrighteousness** (1 John 1:9). God is there to forgive us, so we should get any problems with sin straightened out right away.

Ephesians 4:27 says, **Neither give place to the devil.** When we don't communicate in relationships, we are giving place to the devil. For example, we can listen to thoughts from the enemy and build up all kinds of accusations and cases against our friends. A communication void in relationships can sometimes cause people to think the worst when, in fact, there may really not be a problem at all, other than a lack of communication.

If we are not careful, we can become so full of hurt, strife and bitterness from a perceived case against us that we allow the devil to build a wall between us and our friends. We may even begin to treat our friends as though they are guilty when they're not. In turn, our friends, who aren't aware of the case we've built against them, may react to a perceived hostility on our part. This can all happen when we refuse to communicate.

A woman and her ten-year-old son were Christmas shopping one year. They had always had a good relationship and thoroughly enjoyed each other, but on this day the son exploded and began to behave rudely to his mother. She immediately canceled the rest of the shopping trip and took him to a nearby restaurant. Sitting in front of a cozy fire, they ate and talked about trivial things until the son's anger had passed. Then she gently asked, "Do you want to tell me what's bothering you?"

"You never let me wear my hair the way I want to!" he blurted out.

"Oh? What do you mean?"

"You always tell me how to get it cut."

"Have you ever told me that you wanted a different haircut?"

"Well, no."

"Have you ever told the hairdresser you wanted a different cut?"

"No."

"Do you expect us to be able to read your mind?"

"Yes."

Because they had a history of solid, open communication, they went on to hammer out an agreement that pleased them both. The young son was granted permission to choose his own hairstyle. The mother retained the right to veto his getting a haircut in a style she felt was seriously unattractive, socially inappropriate or damaging to his hair. This mother and son understood the importance of communicating instantly about any issue. Because they canceled everything until the issue was resolved, this situation never damaged their relationship. That son is now in college, and his mother has never had to veto a haircut.

That's what communication is all about—dealing openly and honestly with issues as they arise. *Communication is to a relationship what blood is to life. Without blood, life cannot exist, and without communication, a relationship cannot exist.* Some people still won't talk and deal with issues that challenge their relationships, but I believe many are learning to do so. People are learning that the devil is out to kill, steal and destroy, but Jesus came to give us life. (John 10:10.)

Jesus said, **I am come that they might have life, and that they might have it more abundantly** (John 10:10). The Greek word for *abundantly* in this text means "above the common, superabundant in quantity, superior in quality." That means we don't have to live an inferior life, because in Jesus Christ our lives can be superior. To be sure, undesirable circumstances will come, but we can avail ourselves of the gift of communication and deal with the issues rather than running from them.

Chapter 21

Admit
Your Errors

If we have made an error, if we have blown an opportunity or if we have made a mistake, we need to be big enough to admit it.

There have been times I have had to apologize to my friends because I did something that wasn't good for the relationships. Thank God, I took the responsibility and apologized.

I believe that if we will apologize when we are in error and do what is right, God will give us peace, whether the other person forgives us or not. At least when we admit we've blown it, we're being honest to ourselves and to our friends. Let's face it, we all blow it sometimes. So instead of making matters worse by trying to hide our mistakes, let's come clean and just admit it.

Chapter 22

Find an Answer Before You Point Out the Problem

Each of us has imperfections, difficulties and problems to deal with when relating to another person. However, we usually don't see the idiosyncrasies in others until we've reached a certain depth in the relationship. After that point, things can begin to irritate us. Our friends may talk too much or not enough. They may eat too fast or too slow. They may be too bossy or too placid. They may dress too neatly or too slovenly. There is no end to the things that may irritate us about our friends.

Despite our irritation, we do our friends and ourselves a disservice when we start pointing out faults before we also have solutions to offer to correct those "faults." Do we understand why our friend's shoes are worn out and he looks tired all the time? Perhaps he's putting his children through college and all of his money is going for tuition. Perhaps he's working around the clock to make a living. If so, do you have a solution for him? Can you help his children get better scholarships? Can you help him find a better-paying job? He probably already knows his shoes are worn and that he is tired; he needs solutions, not criticism.

Likewise, we do our churches a disservice when we criticize without offering solutions. Perhaps, for example, you don't like the music at your church. Do you have a solution your pastor has not thought of? Can you help increase the music department's budget so they can afford to do new and different things? Are you willing to volunteer to sing or play an instrument? Can you take care of purchasing the sheet music? How can *you* improve the music at your church?

Problem solving is best done methodically. Here are a few steps that I believe will help you lovingly offer solutions to your friends. I would suggest working through each step before ever pointing out a problem in others.

1. Identify the problem.
2. Try to determine why the problem exists.
3. List all possible solutions.
4. Analyze each solution, studying the costs and consequences of its implementation.
5. Select the best solution for the circumstances.
6. Implement the solution.

By using these steps to solve each problem, you can soon become so accustomed to the process that you do it automatically. You will find that you criticize less, and people will listen more.

Chapter 23

Discover What Your Friends Think of Themselves

Some of our friends may have difficulty communicating with others; they may not always know what to say to people. For example, Sharon and I have been married since 1962, and now there is great communication between us. But when we were first married, Sharon didn't talk much.

After we started having children, she wrapped herself up in them and didn't reach out to me as much. We still had a good relationship, but I began to notice that we were drifting apart a little. Because I was the one who recognized we were growing in different ways, I knew it was my responsibility to try to keep us close together. In order to help our relationship grow closer, I suggested we deal with issues of communication. I made sure we were both growing in the same ways and in the same areas.

After the children grew older and Sharon had more time to devote to herself, she began to read 2 Corinthians 5:21: **For he hath made him to be sin for us, who knew no sin; that we might be made the righteousness of God in him.** Sharon is a beautiful woman, but her inner beauty outshines her exterior beauty. She is good, loving, kind and unassuming—she always has been. But Sharon was insecure, and that's why she didn't talk much. She felt timid in large groups and would not talk because she felt that she didn't know what to say to people.

Consequently, she was accused of being stuck-up. As her husband, I can tell you that Sharon was not, and is not, proud or stuck-up. She was just insecure and, consequently, stayed to herself. She wasn't a person who would go up to someone and start a conversation. She didn't know what to say, and she was afraid of being rejected.

Some people told me, "Boy, Sharon won't talk to us. She thinks she's better than everybody else." Actually, it was the opposite. She thought everybody else was better than she was. That's why she wouldn't talk to them. But when she began to read 2 Corinthians 5:21, she began to realize who she was in Christ. She got tired of living in her shell, and she began to break out. She asked God to send His perfect love to cast out fear, the spirit of intimidation, the spirit of rejection and the feeling of insecurity. She allowed the Spirit of God to heal her. She began to take little steps of faith to overcome that insecurity.

God changed Sharon. She was always a strong woman, but she is much stronger now. She has come out of that shell, and God is using her now to help a lot of people. Sharon's change was not my doing; all I did was love her and pray for her. I didn't push or pull her out of her shell; in fact, had I tried, she probably would have gone in deeper. But God helped Sharon deal with her insecurities through His Word, and she grew up in God.

Because of this experience I had with Sharon, I realized how important it is to discover what people close to me think of themselves. I was able to help Sharon with my love and prayers. Moreover, I learned how to help others once I found out what they thought of themselves.

PART IV

Tip in Advance

Chapter 24

Be Careful With Labels; People Tend To Live Up to Them

It is fairly common for us to try to predict how people will react in a given situation. Unfortunately, however, once we think we know how people will respond, we sometimes label them and tend to treat them accordingly.

For example, years ago there was some discussion about whether public school teachers were treating students fairly. In a study, average students were placed in several classes in which the teachers were told they were dealing with above- average students. Sure enough, the teachers began to treat these students as though they were above average and, amazingly, the students began to act as though they were above average. They lived up to the label that was placed on them.

In the same study, bright students were placed in several classes where the teachers were told they were below-average students. This time, the teachers began to treat them as below average, and their grades began to fall. Soon these bright students began performing poorly. They too, lived up to (or rather down to) the label they were given.

In a book that created quite a stir in the business world a number of years ago, John Malloy demonstrated that people were treated according to the labels they put on themselves. He discussed such things as colors, design of clothes and patterns. In every test, the treatment they received was directly correlated to the *label* they had donned.[1]

When we label people, we tend to treat them accordingly. Unfortunately, if we have given them a bad label, when they see how we are treating them, they live up to the label placed on them. Why do we so often do this? The answer is that we label people according to our perceptions of them. First we draw inferences based on their actions or expressions; then we make judgments; and finally we draw conclusions.

In his book, *Making Friends (& Making Them Count)*, E.M. Griffin lists seven systematic biases that we all seem to share. It is when we exercise these biases that we tend to label others. Let's look at them:

1. We assume others will react to the world just as we do.

2. What we *expect* to see strongly colors what we *do* see.

3. We give undue weight to first impressions.

4. Negative data makes a bigger impact on us than positive information.

5. It's easier to spot others' displeasure than their satisfaction.

6. We attribute more freedom of action to others than they really have.

7. We hold ourselves less responsible for our actions than the situation warrants.[2]

Rarely do others react to the world just as we do. Our differences are colored by the values that have formed our individual natures. As Americans, it is difficult for us to remember that we come from different cultures, but we must keep this in mind if we want to avoid mislabeling people. By recognizing the different cultures people come from, we can see five basic sets of values people adopt:

1. Our view of human nature. (Do we see human nature as evil? mixed? or good?)

2. Our view of the relationship between mankind and God, or between mankind and nature. (Do we value nature over mankind? Do we view nature and mankind as equals? Or do we see mankind as superior to nature?)

3. Our view of time. (Do we dwell on the past? the present? or the future?)

4. Our view of personal growth. (Do we think simply *being* is enough? Must we grow? Or do we strive to be constantly doing something?)

5. Our view of social relationships. (Do we promote authoritarian relationships? group relationships? or individualism?)

The Bias of Assuming Others Will React as We Would

Suppose there were two friends who were brought up differently. One was taught to be ambitious, busy and goal-oriented. The other valued relaxation and spending quality time with people. Would it not be logical that those two friends might label each other? One might label the other as lazy and static, while the other might label his friend as overly ambitious and forward-looking. Well, who's right? Both are.

Remember, relationships aren't about being right or wrong. They're about loving and accepting other people for who they are.

The Bias of Seeing
Exactly What We Expect To See

That which we *expect* to see strongly colors what we *do* see. Reporters and policemen tell us that the obvious frequently goes unnoticed. That's why a man can shave off his mustache or beard without anyone really taking notice. The same thing is true when someone buys a new a pair of glasses or changes hairstyles. We know something is different, but we can't always identify what it is. People rarely notice the mail carrier or the delivery truck driver who constantly drives the same route.

Often we label people by what we think their personalities or mannerisms portray. We tend to label quiet, gentle people as being less assertive and less powerful than loud, boisterous people. In reality, the opposite may be true.

We may label someone a prophet of God, for example, because he or she is forthright, honest and confident. However, the truth may be that he or she is just cantankerous and obnoxious. Conversely, we may label someone as quiet and gentle, when in reality there may be a seething mass of anger and violence beneath that person's quiet surface.

We also often label people based on our expectations of them, rather than objective observations. That's why every mother's child is the smartest, and every father's child is the best.

The Bias of Misreading First Impressions

We often give undue weight to first impressions. In the previously mentioned study about teachers who treated their students differently based on the labels given them, first impressions played a key role in how the teachers responded. First impressions are hard to shake.

The Bias of Accepting Negative
Feedback Over Positive Feedback

Negative data makes a bigger impact on us than positive information. Gossip, weaknesses and doubts seem to be most fascinating to us. For example, some employers gloss over the praises mentioned in letters of recommendation for prospective employees. Rather than focusing on their strengths, interviewers seem to hone in on weaknesses. Gossip always gets somebody's attention. All too often, we form opinions based on negative information, doubts and gossip, thereby labeling people unfairly.

The Bias of Recognizing
Someone's Displeasure Before Pleasure

It's easier to spot others' displeasure than their satisfaction. Ask any married couple, and they may tell you it is much easier to know when their mates are upset about something than to know when they are pleased. I think the reason this happens is that most of us learn very early to read signs of displeasure: wrinkled brows, twitching muscles in the jaw, fire in the eyes, clenched fists, hunched shoulders, folded arms, set mouths or stiffened postures.

On the other hand, we have not taken much time to learn the body language of satisfaction. Additionally, we sometimes erroneously label a person based on body language alone. For example, one woman I know could be labeled as a cross, angry woman because of the wrinkles between her eyebrows when, in fact, she is rarely cross or angry. The wrinkles are caused by unbalanced vision: She is nearsighted in one eye and farsighted in the other.

The Bias of Judging
One Another's Actions Incorrectly

We often think others enjoy more freedom than they really do. Based on superficial appearances, we sometimes tend to misread the motivation behind others' actions. Is the poor man morally superior to the rich man? Or is the rich man better than the poor man? Is the teacher who volunteers nobler than the teacher who needs to be paid?

Is that person's seemingly good fortune the result of determination or mere serendipity? Do the freedom and power that someone uses to make decisions, take action or go somewhere in life come from within, or is that our perception of the freedom and power that person has?

Many times we imagine that someone has a sense of freedom when it may not even exist. Families often fall into this trap as they judge each other and blame others for not phoning, writing, visiting, sending gifts, etc. We think we know the details of our family members' lives, but we usually don't see the whole picture. None of us truly knows the other's motivation for doing something. We can guess or speculate, but only God knows the heart. Yet we tend to label people from our perceptions, which are often completely inaccurate.

The Bias of Holding Ourselves Less Responsible
for Our Actions Than the Situation Warrants

We often hold ourselves less responsible for our actions than the situation warrants. We tend to make excuses for ourselves, while insisting that others take responsibility for all their actions.

I knew a man who made a point of never being responsible for anything. He would not sign for anything; he would not offer an idea in writing; he would not commit to any course of action; he covered every complaint about his services with memos about how the complainer had failed to take responsibility. He labeled all other people as irresponsible, but he was an unhappy man who had no peace; he was too afraid to accept responsibility himself.

In *Maxims for Revolutionists*, George Bernard Shaw wrote, "Liberty means responsibility. That is why most men dread it." Apparently, most of us dislike accepting responsibility, or at least our excuses say we do. We say things like, "Look what you made me do." "That's not my area." "You approved this; it's not my fault." "What about those other people?"

The list goes on and on. But I wonder if we are not giving up some of our liberties when we refuse to accept responsibility. Are we demanding of others what we refuse to do ourselves? Worse than that, are we erroneously labeling people because they act as we act?

How many times in our relationships with others do we relabel others rather than building them up? We say, "Well, this person is going to become angry over that situation." Or, "That person will have something else to say about the matter." If we could only grasp the fact that *people live up to the labels we put on them.* If we must label, then let us start placing positive, healthy, uplifting labels on people. Let us label others as we ourselves would want to be labeled.

Chapter 25

Treat the Person Right and Give All That You've Got

I've discovered that when we treat each person right and give all we've got to relationships, we will prosper. Heaven's floodgates will open for us. We will be blessed in all areas of our lives. You see, when we serve the Lord with all our hearts and quit blaming, finding fault and looking for wrong all the time, we will start living the kind of life God intended for us to live.

The apostle James said, **Don't grumble about each other, brothers. Are you yourselves above criticism? For see! The great Judge is coming. He is almost here. [Let him do whatever criticizing must be done.]** (James 5:9 TLB).

Treating people right is not easy to do, but God very pointedly makes it a requirement of Christian living. Let's look at several Scriptures that deal with this issue.

From 1 Thessalonians 5:14-24 TLB:

- **Comfort those who are frightened.**
- **Take tender care of those who are weak; and be patient with everyone.**
- **See that no one pays back evil for evil, but always try to do good to each other and to everyone else.**
- **Always be joyful.**
- **Always keep on praying.**

- No matter what happens, always be thankful, for this is God's will for you who belong to Christ Jesus.

- Do not scoff at those who prophesy, but test everything that is said to be sure it is true, and if it is, then accept it.

- Keep away from every kind of evil.

- May the God of peace himself make you entirely pure and devoted to God.

From Romans 13:8-10 TLB:

- Pay all your debts except the debt of love for others—never finish paying that! For if you love them, you will be obeying all of God's laws, fulfilling all his requirements.

- If you love your neighbor as much as you love yourself you will not want to harm or cheat him or kill him or steal from him. And you won't sin with his wife or want what is his, or do anything else the Ten Commandments say is wrong. All ten are wrapped up in this one, to love your neighbor as you love yourself.

- Love does no wrong to anyone. That's why it fully satisfies all of God's requirements. It is the only law you need.

From James 3:13-18 TLB:

- If you are wise, live a life of steady goodness, so that only good deeds will pour forth.

- And if you don't brag about them, then you will be truly wise!

- And by all means don't brag about being wise and good if you are bitter and jealous and selfish; that is the worst sort of lie. For jealousy and selfishness are not God's kind of wisdom. Such things are earthly, unspiritual, inspired by the devil.

- For wherever there is jealousy or selfish ambition, there will be disorder and every other kind of evil.
- But the wisdom that comes from heaven is first of all pure and full of quiet gentleness.
- Then it is peace-loving and courteous.
- It allows discussion and is willing to yield to others; it is full of mercy and good deeds.
- It is wholehearted and straightforward and sincere.
- And those who are peacemakers will plant seeds of peace and reap a harvest of goodness.

Did you notice that these Scriptures come with the promise of a harvest of goodness? However, we can only reap that harvest when we learn to treat people right and to give all that we have to each relationship.

Chapter 26

Learn To Tip in Advance

Once I was in a restaurant where only one waitress was on the floor. All of the customers' meals were served late, and some people were not even getting waited on. To top it off, she was rude.

As I sat watching her,

I calculated the time I had remaining before I had to leave. I realized I didn't have enough time to go to another restaurant, but it looked as though I was not going to get service at this restaurant either.

There's got to be a way to change this whole situation, I thought. *I need to get waited on, get my order and get back to the office.* I sat there and thought about the situation for a few moments. Then I had an idea.

I got out of my chair and went to the waitress and asked, "Could I see you just a minute?"

"What'cha want?" she yelled.

Oh, God, what did I just do? I thought. *I have probably blown it.*

But I reached into my pocket and got her a really nice tip and said, "I'm going to tip you in advance." Boy, did that ever change things!

"Oh, sir," she said. Not only did she come to my table, but she started getting all the customers' orders out to them.

The cook looked out the window between the kitchen and the dining room and asked, "What happened to her?" He couldn't believe the change that had taken place.

But what would have happened if I had taken on her wrong spirit? It would have become a mess. Sadly, that's what we do sometimes when we hang around someone who is hurting and lashing out at others. Very often we join them in that same wrong spirit. I don't want to walk in the wrong spirit; I want to walk in love.

As I watched her change, I thought, *She might be a single mother with three or four kids at home. She might be paying all the bills, while expecting child support that never comes. Who knows what that woman is going through?*

Finally someone came over to my table and asked, "What did you do?"

"I tipped her in advance," I said.

"You what?"

"I tipped her in advance."

I've learned to tip in advance in my relationships too. I learned this years ago from Sharon. When we would be preparing to go to bed, she would go in and remove the decorative pillows, take the bedspread off, fold it and then turn the covers down. Then all we had to do was get into bed, pull the sheets and blanket over us and go to sleep.

But sometimes I would go to bed early, since I'm an early riser. I particularly like to get up early and pray. (I've practiced this for years. Many times before my wife is awake, I am up and praying.) And when I would go to bed early, I would just pull back the spread a little, push the pillows and things over to Sharon's side, slip between the sheets and go to sleep.

One day Sharon asked, "Don, have you ever noticed that if I go to bed first, or when we go to bed together I remove the spread and fold it, turn the covers down and fluff the pillows? That way you can just slip into bed and enjoy the comfort. Have you ever noticed that?"

"Yes," I said, "I really like it when you arrange the covers before we go to bed."

"Well, why don't you do this for me?"

"Well, Sharon, I've never thought about it."

Then it dawned on me that I should treat her the way I want to be treated. I should do for her what she does for me—and even more.

That night I went to bed early. I pulled the spread back, folded it just the way she did and put it away. I fixed the blanket, folded back the covers and fluffed the pillows. I went into the bathroom, got her perfume and began to spray it lightly over the bed. When she came in she said, "Oh, I see you've changed." And what a positive change it was! Instead of expecting something to be done for me, I started doing what she did for me; and it made a big difference.

That's the kind of advance tipping I'm talking about. If we'll tip up front in our relationships, we'll see wondrous changes. Go ahead and give people kind words. Don't wait until they earn them. Say something nice even before you think they deserve it.

If we'll treat our friends this way and actually do what the Bible says, we will receive blessings in our relationships that we've never dreamed of.

Do nothing from factional motives—through contentiousness, strife, selfishness or for unworthy ends—or prompted by conceit and empty arrogance. Instead, in the true spirit of humility (lowliness of mind) let each regard the others as better than and superior to himself—thinking more highly of one another than you do of yourselves. Let each of you esteem and look upon and be concerned for not [merely] his own interests, but also each for the interests of others.

Philippians 2:3,4 AMP

If we show interest in others, they will feel important. Furthermore, if we keep our motives pure and unselfish, it will be like tipping up front. Then we can watch and see the blessings of God come into our lives.

PART V

Learn the Difference Between Giving and Receiving

Chapter 27

Once You Give, It's No Longer Yours

Have you ever noticed that it's frequently in our close, intimate relationships that we get hurt the most? That's why it's important for us to remember not to always react emotionally and attempt to defend ourselves. Sometimes we can lose friends if we refuse to accept some of the blame or admit any personal wrongdoing.

I've entered into some relationships knowing that once I started them, I was going to be the one responsible for making them work. These are difficult relationships to sustain. Looking back, I should have asked myself, *Why do I want this relationship? Do I even want this person in my life?*

Had I known then what I know now, I never would have gotten into those dysfunctional relationships, which is exactly what they were. Perhaps I got into them at the time to satisfy an inner need that only God could have met. Nevertheless, I was hurt in nearly every one of those relationships because I gave something of myself but received nothing in return.

We should not enter into one-sided relationships like that. It's unhealthy to hold on to relationships in which we're continually walking on eggshells, wondering if the relationship is going to survive tomorrow.

One of the biggest problems we can have in our relationships is that, even though we may be walking in the Spirit, we expect things from people who sometimes aren't even aware that we have a need. We may think, *Well, if they were close enough to God, they would know my need.* But that thinking indicates selfishness. We should never expect our friends to meet all of our needs.

We should always try to make quality decisions when giving our friendship to individuals; but once we have given friendship to another person, it's not ours any longer. It's rather like giving an offering to God through a ministry or church—just give it. Don't try to tell someone what to do with the offering, because it's not yours to control.

This reminds me of the time someone wanted to give me a gift. My friend said, "Don, we want to give you this gift, but we don't want you to give it away."

"What?" I asked.

"We're going to give you this, but we know how you are, always giving things away. And we don't want you to give this away."

"I'm sorry, but I cannot receive this gift on those terms," I said.

"Yes, you can," my friend said. "We just don't want you to give it away."

"If you give it to me as a gift, it shouldn't matter what I do with it, because you're giving it to me to do with it what I want to. When you give it to me, it's mine; it's no longer yours. And if it's mine, you can't direct it any longer."

It's the same way in some relationships. Sometimes we want to give people our love, but we also want to tell them how to handle it. When we do this, we are trying to control the relationship. But once you give your love, it's given. Love is not love until you give it away. Then it's gone. But God's Word says

He is faithful to give it back to us. **Give, and it shall be given unto you; good measure, pressed down, and shaken together, and running over, shall men give into your bosom. For with the same measure that ye mete withal it shall be measured to you again** (Luke 6:38).

Another pit into which some people fall is expecting gratitude in return for a gift. When we see someone who is down and out and needs our help, we can offer our assistance. But after we've helped, that person may forget to show us gratitude. He or she may even write us off. But if we've helped someone out of love, we should not expect anything in return. Gratitude should not be the basis for our giving. If, however, we do receive gratitude, let us consider it a bonus.

Never remember what you do for someone else, but never forget what they do for you. What truth there is in this statement! Had I discovered this earlier in my life, I would have been spared a lot of pain. I have tried to live my life helping people and giving them great opportunities; I've helped get doors opened for people who have enjoyed great success, although sometimes they've later acted as if I never existed. There have been times when I could have used some help in return, but they chose not to help me. They totally forgot the time, love and commitment I had invested in them.

Many times, I've helped people become acquainted or I've helped them get back together again, and I've done it without expecting anything in return. Usually, after they've met and developed a relationship, these people no longer needed my help. This used to bother me, but then I understood I was supposed to introduce them. It was part of their destiny to meet. However, in the past, I got hurt and offended over this. Since then, God has helped me to grow past this and to recognize that they don't owe me anything for what I did. So now when I help people, I do it because I know that is one of God's plans for my life, and I should not expect anything in return.

God taught me to release people and showed me that they don't owe me anything. The important thing is not their response; the important thing is *my obedience.* God is the One who brings back to me what I need, whether in the form of relationships or open doors. He always honors my obedience.

When we help someone, we are not to expect anything in return. We are to free people and let them soar. Keep in mind that God sees what we do; it won't go unrewarded. We are told in Genesis 1:11 that every seed produces after its own kind. In Galatians 6:7, we are told that whatever we sow, we will reap. If you help others and they forget about it, don't worry. God doesn't forget. The Bible says, **The eyes of the Lord are in every place, beholding the evil and the good** (Prov. 15:3). We must guard our emotions at all times and, as Ephesians 4:27 says, give no place to the devil. For he will use any incident he can to cause us to stumble.

Though it may be tempting to respond emotionally when we face this type of situation in reality, we must protect our hearts, for **out of it are the issues of life** (Prov. 4:23). If we keep the issues of life pure and holy, even if we've been let down, then we can fully trust God to restore us. God said in Hebrews 13:5, **I will never leave thee, nor forsake thee.** We should remember what others do for us and forget what we do for others.

Chapter 28

Understand the Principles of Giving

As stated in the previous chapter, a freely given gift should not be followed by unrealistic expectations of any kind. The giving of a gift should not allow the giver to control the recipient, nor should it allow the giver to control how the recipient uses the gift. If it does, then it's not a gift but a debt.

A gift becomes the possession of the recipient; the giver has relinquished all rights to it. The recipient now has the right to use or dispose of the gift in any way he or she sees fit. He may choose to destroy it, put it in the trash, give it away, put it away or never use or even display it; none of this should matter to the giver.

The only exception to this rule I can think of is when the sentimental value of a gift is the greatest part of the gift. In this case, the giver should state his or her expectations up front and allow the recipient the opportunity to accept or refuse the terms of the gift.

For example, after Sharon's mother died, Sharon inherited items belonging to her mother that she could not use herself. Because of this, Sharon wanted to give them to someone who would appreciate them. I believe she had the right to seek someone who could value these deeply sentimental gifts. She would ask her friends, "If you don't want this, please don't accept it," or, "If you are going to get rid of it, please give it back to me."

At that point, the recipients, recognizing that this was a gift representing Sharon's memories, had to decide whether or not they wanted the gift under those terms. Sharon, on the other hand, knew she would have to release her hold on the gift, recognizing that even though the recipient had agreed to her request, it might not be carried out.

Hopefully, the recipient in such an instance will use wisdom and do the right thing with the gift. But once the giver presents it to the other person, he loses all rights over the gift. If the giver tries to control it, then he never releases the gift in the first place. The blessing that comes to the giver is not based on what the recipient does with the gift; the blessing is based on the motives of the giver. So when one gives a gift, he should release it and expect God to bless him, regardless of what the recipient does with it.

Not all gifts are wrapped in special paper and tied with ribbons. Some gifts, such as generosity, kindness or love can be powerful influences in people's lives. They can even be returned to us with the same generosity in which we gave them, according to the purity of our motives.

In addition, gifts can open doors to people of influence, but the giver should not use a gift to buy favors or influence. I've given gifts to some people and seen relationships develop (at least I thought they were developing), until I stopped giving gifts. Suddenly all communications ceased on their parts, and I realized they didn't want relationships; they wanted the gifts.

This happened to me several times. As a result, I learned that no matter who I give to, if I keep my motives pure and expect nothing in return, God will give back to me one way or another. Now when I give a gift, rather than placing expectations on the recipient, I let God open the door, granting me favor.

Giving and Tithing

A gift in the form of a tithe or offering is given to God through your local church, the institution that represents God on earth. Obviously, you need to use wisdom when you give to ministries and charities. Pray over your tithes and offerings, giving only to those ministries possessing character and integrity, those which have track records of doing what they say.

If a ministry you do give to does not use the money as they've indicated, remember that you've given to God, not to a ministry or charity. Let God handle the situation. In the meantime, consider whether or not you really heard from God about giving the gift. Perhaps you gave out of an emotional response. If you did, learn the lesson and refuse to become bitter about it. In the future, concentrate on hearing from God regarding where He wants you to correctly place the gift.

Jesus promised a return on our giving from the heart: **Give, and it shall be given unto you; good measure, pressed down, and shaken together, and running over, shall men give into your bosom. For with the same measure that ye mete withal it shall be measured to you again** (Luke 6:38).

This Scripture plainly promises a return, but it does not indicate from which source the return will come. It doesn't say the recipient will give back to the giver. If our motives for giving are right, God will work through *someone* to return our gifts in full measure. Look at Luke 6:35 TLB:

Love your enemies! Do good to them! Lend to them! And don't be concerned about the fact that they won't repay. Then your reward from heaven will be very great, and you will truly be acting as sons of God: for he is kind to the unthankful and to those who are very wicked.

Many times people miss their blessings because their motives and attitudes are wrong; they expect the gift to earn them influence or favor from the recipient. It may do just that, but if earned favor is the motive for the giving, then it's not a gift but a deal. If the giver's motive is to make a deal, usually he or she gets hurt or offended when the recipient doesn't meet the expectation.

As a pastor, I've heard many stories about people's giving practices. I've also heard that people sometimes ask for things to be returned after they've been given. That's not really a gift; that's a loan. When one gives, one does not have the right to ask for the gift back.

It's important to qualify the reason and motive for giving. Those who truly give realize the gift is no longer theirs. They no longer have any claim on the gift because they gave it to God.

One day while I was walking through the church, I overheard several people talking about using a room for a ministry function. One person said, "We tithe here so we have a right to use this room." Of course that got my attention, and I addressed the situation. Well, as it turned out, those people did not appreciate what I had to say and they eventually left the church. They said, "If we tithe here, we should have a vote and a voice."

That's not what the Bible teaches. The Word says that the tithe belongs to God. (Mal. 3:8.) It never did belong to the person giving it. The person giving the tithe is there to channel the tithe to God, not to control the use of the tithe. God's Word is plain; God will rebuke the devourer because of your obedience. (v. 11.) Once you've given your tithe, the church does not owe you anything; it is God who makes the promise to repay. (v. 10.)

> "Bring all the tithes into the storehouse, that there may be food in My house, and try Me now in this," says the Lord of hosts, "if I will not open for you the windows of heaven and pour out for you such blessing that there will not be room enough to receive it. And I will rebuke the devourer for your sakes, so that he will not destroy the fruit of your ground, nor shall the vine fail to bear fruit for you in the field," says the Lord of hosts.
>
> Malachi 3:10,11 NKJV

Let's look at another Scripture and shed some more light on this subject:

> "Woe to you, scribes and Pharisees, hypocrites! For you pay tithe of mint and anise and cummin, and have neglected the weightier matters of the law: justice and mercy and faith. These you ought to have done, without leaving the others undone."
>
> Matthew 23:23 NKJV

In Mathew 23:23, Jesus was talking to the leaders of a synagogue, telling them to pay attention to their work. From this we can see that God holds leaders accountable for their followers. Therefore, if you're a member of a church and you're being fed there, you should tithe to that church and love God, the pastor and the people. Then believe *God* for the increase in your life. You should not tell the leadership how to spend money. Neither should you become angry because someone didn't take your advice or do something your own way.

Remember, the tithe is the Lord's, not yours. Again, the pastor should be a person of character and integrity but, unfortunately, we all know that not all people who claim to be servants of God walk with integrity. Of course, I'm not advocating giving to the wrong projects or people, but the real issues are the motive of the heart and the expectation put on the gift.

Recognition for Going Above and Beyond the Call of Duty

Sometimes people receive a gift or bonus for having done an excellent job. A bonus is something extra that is given. It is not necessarily promised, it is not commissioned and it is not negotiated. Since it is something extra, it should be received with gratitude and thankfulness toward God. Sadly, instead of showing gratitude, some people complain, "See, I told you my boss was cheap; he could have been paying me more all the time. I deserve more for all I do, and this is all they think of me." This kind of attitude will quickly sour any relationship with an employer.

One subject that can lead to quarrels between employers and their employees is the giving of Christmas bonuses. This practice often lends itself to unbalanced expectations. For some people, no bonus is ever enough. No matter what the amount of the bonus, these people tend to expect a larger bonus each year. But that's not the right attitude. Employees should not automatically expect a larger gift from an employer just because he received a gift the year before.

How many people ever take the time to show appreciation for the Christmas bonuses that they do receive? How many people write thank-you notes to their employers? Instead of complaining about the amount they receive, they should show gratitude. When employees take time to show gratitude to their employers and to God, they're walking in agreement with the Word of God. By showing gratitude, people strengthen relationships and open greater doors for blessings.

Our Incomes Are a Gift From God

Even though we work for it, our incomes are, in a sense, gifts from God through our employers. I've gone places to speak and been compensated far less than what I had expected and needed. But instead of complaining about it, I put the situation in the hands of the Lord and was grateful for what I did receive. When this happens now, because of my grateful attitude toward God, God supplies my needs.

For example, when I was younger, I spoke at a church for three weeks, and we had great meetings. It was the pastor's practice to wait until the close of the meetings to give me my portion of the offerings. And when he finally did give me my part, I found it was not anything close to what he had promised. I had personally received the offerings during each meeting, and I knew that much more had been taken in than what he had given me represented. I was hurt and said something to him about it, but he told me they were collecting for a building fund and that he needed it more than I did. Although this hurt me, I turned it all over to God, and God met my needs in another way.

On another occasion, at the end of the service at another church, a pastor gave me a check, which I could tell he did not really want to give. Without even looking at the check, I smiled at him and said, "You need this more than I do."

He took the check back and said, "You're right."

I kept a good attitude, and God met my need in another way. I am glad my wife and I have learned to trust God instead of people.

Use Integrity With Expense Accounts

Expense accounts are gifts designated for a specific purpose. My dad always taught me to be honest and to treat other people right, handling their belongings as though they were my own. This may seem silly to some people, but I'm talking about heart issues, whether large or small, that affect relationships. For example, I've gone out to eat with people who were using an expense account and they ordered the most expensive items from the menu, items they would never have ordered had they been paying for the meal themselves. I have a problem with that practice.

If you had an expense account and you were given carte blanche to spend it, perhaps it would be acceptable to order the most expensive items on menus. But it is wrong to indulge oneself at another person's expense. I believe we should spend other people's money the same way we would our own.

During the early years of my ministry, I suffered some financial hardships. Many times, my wife and I had to sacrifice a lot. Sometimes we slept in our car, and often we ate at the cheapest places in town. However, as God began to bless us, we could afford to stay at better places and eat in nicer restaurants. When we first began to stay at hotels with room service, we didn't use the service because it would cost more. At the time, it was wisdom for us to save the extra dollars.

When a church would put us in a hotel at their expense, we still didn't order room service. The reason we didn't use room service was simple. We wouldn't have used room service had we been paying for it ourselves. So out of a sense of integrity, we didn't use it when they were paying for it either.

However, when I reached a point where I could afford room service at hotels, then and only then did I accept room service from the church that was covering my expenses. When I could afford it myself, I felt free to accept it from the church. I always did what I could do with my own money. To me, this is another issue of the heart.

In Luke 16:10-12, Jesus stressed the importance of exercising honesty in small issues:

> **"He that is faithful in that which is least is faithful also in much: and he that is unjust in the least is unjust also in much. If therefore ye have not been faithful in the unrighteous mammon, who will commit to your trust the true riches? And if ye have not been faithful in that which is another man's, who shall give you that which is your own?"**

God has provided for my family because I've always tried to treat people and the things they entrust to me in a way I would want them to treat me or my things. For example, if I borrow a car, I return it sparkling clean and with more gas than it had when I got it. Honesty, even in the small issues, is the bedrock of relationships.

Discounts Are for Customers

Discounts are gifts that businesses choose to give to customers. It bothers me when someone *expects* a discount from a Christian businessperson merely because they both happen to be Christians. I think the opposite should be true. I think Christians should want to pay full price to Christian businesspeople so they will have more to give back into the kingdom of God.

If Christian businesspeople want to give a discount, that's up to them. But I don't think Christians should expect a discount just because they are Christians.

Always Keep Your Word

Keeping one's word is a gift of commitment. I've watched relationships become destroyed because one believer took a job with another believer and would not do the job he committed to do. When one person tells another what he or she will do for a certain amount of money, then it should be done to the best of that person's ability. Each person should honor his or her word.

Punctuality: A Gift of Respect

Punctuality is a gift of respect. In any relationship, it is important to be sensitive and show respect for others in matters of punctuality. For example, when a person is habitually late, causing others to wait on him or her, that person is not only showing disrespect but is also controlling the others' time.

Some people are never on time and will probably never change. This practice is dishonorable and disrespectful. Those same people would probably become really angry if others were late keeping appointments with them.

As a pastor, I see people who are always late to church. They usually have an excuse, but the excuse only satisfies the one giving it. If the church service runs longer than usual, those same people are usually the ones who complain the loudest. I once knew some people who always came in to church about fifteen to thirty minutes late. At noon they walked out, even if the service was not yet over. Their actions showed no respect for the church, for the leaders or for God.

Refusing To Argue Is a Gift of Patience

No one wins in an argument that is fraught with emotions. Even though one person may be better and quicker with words, he does not necessarily win the argument. No matter what the outcome, the other person can continue to think whatever he wants to.

When two people are in an emotional argument, no one really wins, because one person takes a superior position over the other and forces them into an inferior position. Both parties lose respect for one another, and ultimately no one wins. Most arguments are lost because one person does not prefer his brother to himself. (Phil. 2:3).

Refuse To Take Offense

Refusing to take offense at something is a gift of freedom you give to yourself. How you leave one relationship is how you will enter the next one. I see this all the time. People come to a church, take offense at someone or something and then leave. Usually they're suspicious of the people they've left behind, and they keep everyone at arm's length. They think the same thing might happen all over again. And it will, if they don't get rid of the offense. Going to another church will not rid them of their problems. An offense like this will shadow them until they deal with it.

The Bible says, **And when ye stand praying, forgive, if ye have aught against any: that your Father also which is in heaven may forgive you your trespasses** (Mark 11:25). By refusing to take offense, we set our own spirits free.

PART VI

Control Your Expectations

Chapter 29

Don't Expect Gratitude

Jesus, who recognized the value of lasting relationships, taught us the way we should treat others. **Therefore all things whatsoever ye would that men should do to you, do ye even so to them: for this is the law and the prophets** (Matt. 7:12). We are commanded to treat others right, regardless of how they treat us. This principle does not promise us that the person we are kind to will be kind in return. What that principle does guarantee, however, is that *someone*—not necessarily the individual in question—will treat us right.

Treating people right includes reaching a mutual understanding at the beginning of the relationship as to what is expected from each party. For example, if I'm making an agreement to perform a service for someone, such as picking up his or her kids from school, I should ask up front what is expected of me. Under these circumstances, whenever I perform this service, it's a deal, not a gift. On the other hand, if I'm doing a kind deed or giving a gift above and beyond the agreement, then I should expect nothing in return.

You see, when we expect something in return for our good deeds, we are setting ourselves up for disappointment, hurt or strained relationships. We should give to our friends as unto the Lord. That's what Paul wrote in Colossians.

> **And whatsoever ye do, do it heartily, as to the Lord, and not unto men; knowing that of the Lord ye shall receive the reward of the inheritance: for ye serve the Lord Christ.**
>
> **Colossians 3:23,24**

One of the greatest lessons I ever learned was not to expect gratitude from favors I provide for my friends. When I first began to pastor, I didn't understand this principle. I expected people to be grateful just for the input I contributed to their lives. I thought they would come to church just because I did kind things for them.

Boy, was I wrong! I got my first eye-opener after making hospital visits. People would call and ask me to visit them or their families and friends in the hospital, so I would drive all over town, going from hospital to hospital visiting people. Sometimes the people I went to see didn't even want to see me. I was there merely to fulfill someone else's request.

After doing this for a while, I thought, *Of all the people I've visited in the hospital, not one has ever come to the church. This is not right!* Then the Lord asked me a question that really got my attention. *Why did you go visit and pray with all those people? Was it to get them healed or to get them to come to church?*

The truth was that I had gone for both reasons. But I was deeply disappointed that none of the people I ever prayed for came to church, as I had expected they would. I had to rethink this issue and reexamine my motives. I came to realize that if I went to pray for someone, I had to do it with love and with no strings attached. I had no right to expect these people to come to my church. How they responded was their choice.

Another difficult area for me was pastoral counseling. I would spend hours and hours with people—listening, encouraging, giving godly advice from the Scriptures and praying. Then, if they didn't get exactly what they expected, they would leave the church.

I remember one man in particular. I counseled him for some time. One day he called for an appointment, but I couldn't see him as soon as he wanted. To make matters worse, my assistant forgot to inform him of the situation. Well, some time later, he scheduled another appointment to tell me he was leaving our church to go to a church where the pastor would care for him.

The truth is that I did care. I cared about this man, but I am only human; I have limited time, and I make mistakes. But I keep on learning. From this experience, I learned that I had to let go of individuals and not let their actions affect my attitude toward others in the church. I learned that I had to turn people over to the caring hands of God. Jesus is their Savior, not I.

Nevertheless, people who lacked loyalty to the church upset me for a long time. I remember loving various people and standing with them when things went wrong and they were hurting. But I was disappointed when they later showed no gratitude or loyalty.

I've poured myself out for members of my congregation. For example, I've stayed at hospitals all day long with folks to comfort and support the families of those who were undergoing major surgeries. I've married their children and buried their dead. But the days have come when some of these same people have become disappointed because things at church have not gone the way they've wanted or they've felt I was incapable of giving them what they've wanted at the moment. Sure enough, they have gone somewhere else.

Recently, a couple who came to visit told me they felt hurt because of their pastor's actions. They felt their pastor had neglected them despite all the things they had done for him and the church. As I questioned them, I found out why they felt hurt. They told me that although a close family member was ill, neither the pastor nor his associate had called, visited or offered prayer. Actually, someone from the church had called, but it was only to ask for help on a special project at the church.

That phone call stirred up their anger.

"Someone from the church can call and ask us for money," they told me, "but no one can even ask how we are! We just can't believe this! We are never going back to that church. We have been going there all these years, and after all we have done, our pastor doesn't think enough of us to even call to see how we're doing!"

I knew they had a valid point, and I could understand how they could be upset by this. But I had to ask them if they were willing to throw away all those good years because of one distasteful incident. I asked them, "Perhaps your pastor doesn't know about your need. Maybe he's caught in a crisis of his own right now. Or maybe his perception of this situation is much different from reality." A lengthy conversation followed.

You see, people need to be heard. So I listened to them, and afterward asked, "Now, are you really going to leave because you got offended once? I realize you're offended because you didn't get what you expected, but are you really going to leave this church because of it? You really shouldn't leave while you're offended. You should get yourself straightened out first and then go. Because if you leave offended, you'll carry that offense with you to the next church, and you won't trust your next pastor either. Furthermore, if God hasn't released you and called you to go somewhere else, then you'll be out of the will of God."

They calmed down after a while and began to remember some of the good times they had had at the church with the pastor. After some time had passed, the family member recovered, and they got over most of their hurt and went back to church. Not long afterward, they were asked to participate in a pastor-appreciation day. That's when I heard from them again. In a panic, they phoned me, asking, "What should we say?"

"The truth," I replied. "First, prepare yourselves by forgiving him for the one time he let you down when your family member was ill. Then, talk about the good times and the good things you remember. Tell the people what this pastor has taught you from the Word of God."

As they made their plans to speak and began thinking about the good things in the relationship, their hearts began to change. They realized how good they had it at that church and how they had almost thrown away a good relationship because of one forgivable failure. They understood again that they belonged at that church and were glad they had decided not to leave.

That pastor-appreciation day was a success because these people were able to work through their pain. Instead of focusing on their pain, they focused on their pastor's true heart.

The devil will use anything he can to break up relationships, whether in the church, the home or between friends. Sadly, his most powerful weapon is often to influence us to take offense instead of examining the hearts of others.

Right and Wrong Expectations in Friendship

Very often, we get our expectations dashed because people don't acknowledge the gifts we give them. More and more, it is becoming commonplace to fail to send thank-you notes or to acknowledge acts of kindness. Negligence in this area seems to extend to all areas.

Certainly people should be courteous enough to acknowledge gifts and responsible enough to follow through with appropriate expressions of gratitude. However, people may neglect this common courtesy for a number of reasons. For instance, one might simply forget. Another might tell someone else to take care of it (sadly, some people have never been taught to say thank you for themselves).

For whatever reason people forget to acknowledge our acts of kindness, we must remember to disconnect our giving from the recipients' responses. When we give, we should expect nothing in return. We do not want to lose God's gifts for our giving just because people aren't courteous to us.

I was taught to be courteous, to say please and thank you, and to show kindness in return for kindness. Because of my training, I expected people to treat me the same way. Unfortunately, this did not always happen.

Earlier in my ministry, I would do things for people and keep tabs on what I had done. And when they would forget to show gratitude, I would get frustrated. At the time, I didn't know this was wrong; I thought they were the ones in the wrong for being ungrateful. I experienced a lot of frustration.

Looking back, I can see that before I learned to look at things from God's perspective, I did things that hampered some of my relationships. The following examples from my experience will illustrate how our negative attitudes can affect our relationships.

Keeping Others in Debt to Us

In the 60s and 70s, I traveled across the United States with a tent revival group. My younger brother Norman worked as my road manager during this time. Once, during a successful crusade in Washington, D.C., I returned to the tent after the evening service to spend some time in prayer. When I left the tent, I found Norman and told him I sensed we should keep his men on duty during the night to avoid having someone steal the equipment.

Without even thinking about it, Norman replied, "I'll personally stay up and watch." So I drove back to the hotel and went to bed. The next morning, as I drove onto the grounds for the morning service, Norman was waiting for me. I could tell by his expression that something was wrong.

"Last night after you left," Norman began, "I went into my trailer for just a few minutes and sat down on the couch. I didn't mean to, but I fell asleep. When I woke up, I immediately ran into the tent and found that all the public address equipment was gone. Apparently, right after I fell asleep, someone came and took everything. I'm so sorry I let you down."

"After all I've done for you, how could you let this happen?" I demanded of him.

Norman's face fell, and his eyes became solemn as we both recalled what had happened several years earlier. Norman had needed a favor, and I had helped him with my influence and contacts. I had offered my help to him as a gift, but every time he made a mistake I reminded him of that favor. I really wasn't doing it intentionally, of course, but I was hurting him anew each time I mentioned it. Lack of gratitude had nothing to do with this situation, for Norman had thanked me repeatedly for my assistance. I was wrongfully using the gift in order to keep him in my debt.

Now, several years later, several hundred people were waiting under the tent for the beginning of the service. And we had no public address system. I still found myself holding Norman's feet to the fire of forced gratitude instead of focusing on the upcoming service.

With tears in his eyes, Norman said, "Don, I know I made a terrible mistake, especially after you cautioned me about feeling that someone was going to take some of the equipment. I feel bad that I let this happen. I know I didn't do my job, but how long am I going to pay for the favor you did for me a couple of years ago? Every time I make a mistake, you bring this up. How can I repay you? Am I going to be in debt to you the rest of my life? If so, I wish you had never helped me!"

His comments hit me between the eyes. Stunned, I got out of the car and threw my arms around him. "Norman, I'm so sorry for what I've done to you. Please forgive me. I will never mention this again." Norman forgave me, and I've never mentioned that incident again. As a result, we've had a wonderful relationship ever since.

The apostle Paul wrote, **Owe no one anything except to love one another, for he who loves another has fulfilled the law** (Rom. 13:8 NKJV). I've had far less stress since I learned not to keep track of what I do for others or to expect gratitude from them, because God is the One who will reward me for my giving. My focus must be on Him.

What Are You Remembering?

Solomon wrote, "Above all else guard your heart, for it affects everything you do." (Prov. 4:23). Several years ago, I met someone who had been greatly used by God but who had fallen into financial troubles. The Lord impressed me to help him with financial support for a short while. So I did. I was happy to assist him, and I did it with no strings attached.

One day as I rode my Harley down the highway, the Lord reminded me that when this person got back on his feet I should not expect him to show me any gratitude. Nor was I to use his influence to help me. I thought to myself, *I know not to expect anything. I'll be all right.*

I supported him for two years, and during that time there was constant communication between us. But by the end of the second year, I felt he'd recovered enough financially for me to stop supporting him. So I stopped supporting him. And, after the support stopped, the communication also stopped.

I'd known this would happen one day, and I'd thought I would be okay with it. I had really thought our relationship was genuine and not based on my supporting his ministry. Therefore, it hurt when he broke fellowship.

Then the Lord reminded me what He'd told me while I was riding the Harley. And because of that word, I was able to guard my heart. But had I not guarded my heart, this experience would have opened a door for disappointment. I could have held him in debt, as I had done to Norman, but God helped me to release him, setting both of us free. When we agree to help someone and expect to be repaid, we should tell the person up front. When we give a gift, though, we should make it a real gift and let it be free of obligation.

You Owe Me a Favor

Relationships are often destroyed because one person believes another owes him a favor. The confusion begins with one's attitude toward giving. A true gift is an act of kindness that has no strings attached. The recipient owes the giver nothing—not even a favor. A loan, on the other hand, requires something in return—whether favors, interest, full or partial repayment, etc.

I was talking with a minister once about his child's upcoming wedding. He said, "The wedding is going to be big, and it's going to be good. I know my child will get plenty of good gifts because a lot of people owe me favors for what I've done for them in the past." I was shocked to hear those words, because I thought he gave to God and not to man.

It's natural to want people to celebrate events in our children's lives, but if they don't send gifts, we shouldn't get offended. God is our source.

Another person told me about giving quite a bit of money to an individual who never acknowledged the gift. The recipient felt like God was supplying his need, so he thanked God, thinking that was all that was necessary. But the giver expected some kind of acknowledgment. And when he didn't receive it, he was offended and vowed to never again give anything to that individual.

In my opinion, both the giver and the recipient made mistakes. The giver should have realized he was giving to God, not man. Likewise, the recipient should have known God was using the giver to supply his needs, and he should have expressed his gratitude to both God and the giver.

Harboring unrealistic expectations, though, can blind one to the truth and prevent one from expressing the proper gratitude. For example, one pastor I know invited a guest minister and his team to his church to speak, and God used the guest minister to touch many people. During his stay, the guest minister was courteous and attentive to the pastor and his wife and spent quite some time ministering to them. At the end of the meeting, the guest minister was even impressed to return a portion of the offering he received to the pastor.

Now, instead of being grateful, the pastor declared he wasn't going to host any more guest speakers. He was afraid the people had come only to see the guest minister and would not return afterwards.

This pastor was offended because he didn't get what he wanted out of the meeting—a larger congregation. In fact, he overlooked the fact that a family who had been out of church for twenty years had rededicated their lives to God during that meeting. That pastor also failed to consider that a number of people in his congregation had been helped.

Perhaps, if this pastor had given it some time, some of the visitors would have returned for another visit. Realistically, this pastor's main desire should have been to allow the guest speaker to minister to his church, teaching them more of the Word and encouraging them to evangelize to the lost.

Ministry is about giving, not getting. There is a return for what we give, but we must put things in perspective before we can expect blessings from God. The Bible says, **All this newness of life is from God, who brought us back to himself through what Christ did, and God has given us the task of reconciling people to him** (2 Cor. 5:18).

Put the Interests of Others First

Expressing appropriate gratitude ceases to be a problem when we put the interests of others first. My wife and I are fortunate to have longtime friends standing by us. But we didn't strive to make these relationships happen. God just provided them for us. We had godly favor, and God placed us in the right place at the right time to make divine connections with certain people. From there, we've sown love and kindness into these relationships over the years.

We've always understood that we should give unto our friends. We didn't do this with ulterior motives, expecting to get something in return. We just wanted to be a blessing.

You see, to enjoy rich, productive relationships, you must put the interests of others first. You can't enter into a relationship expecting to automatically receive something. Likewise, you can't run the moment you don't get something your way. This opens the door to frustration and a broken relationship. First, begin to trust the other person, and then start looking for and encouraging his or her strengths.

A good question to ask at the outset of any relationship with someone is *Why do I want a relationship with this person?*

For example, are you getting into a relationship because someone has something you want, and you think that by getting close enough you can get what you need? Do you form relationships with others because they're well-known and you want to gain recognition for yourself? Maybe you seek people out for relationships because you think they can help you network with others.

Just remember, a genuine relationship is always based on pure motives, not unrealistic expectations and selfishness. The Bible says, **Do nothing out of selfish ambition or vain conceit, but in humility consider others better than yourselves. Each of you should look not only to your own interests, but also to the interests of others** (Phil. 2:3,4 NIV).

Sharon and I experienced this biblical principle in action once when we reached out to a neighbor.

One Christmas, when we lived in Chattanooga, Tennessee, we met a neighbor we wanted to bless. He had been kind, greeting us out in our yard, and we liked him. So we bought him a gift one day and took it to his house. He very graciously invited us in, and we explained to him that we just wanted to say "Merry Christmas" and give him a gift.

"But I didn't buy you anything," he said.

We chuckled and said, "We weren't expecting anything. We just wanted to give you a Christmas gift." So we gave him the gift and after a few minutes went back home.

A couple of days went by, and we received a call from this man. He said he wanted to take us to dinner. Although I didn't think about it at the time, he said he felt obligated to do something for us because of the gift. Naturally, we accepted his invitation without thinking anything of it.

When we arrived at the restaurant, I went to the waiter and asked that I be given the bill. Now, our neighbor had no idea that I did this. Well, we enjoyed a pleasant dinner, and afterward I arranged to pay the bill. Still, our neighbor knew nothing about this. So at the end of the meal, he asked for the check and was shocked to learn it had already been paid.

He was beside himself, saying, "No preacher has ever bought my dinner."

"Now one has," I said.

Well, eventually we left and went our separate ways, but he called in a couple of days. He said, "I've been thinking about the gifts you gave me, and now I want to know what you want?"

"Nothing," I said.

"You must want something, and I sure would like to know what it is. I owe you now, and I don't like being in debt to anyone."

"No, you don't owe me anything," I responded. "I told you it was a gift."

"Let me pay you back."

"You can't pay back a gift; just accept it."

Well, he finally did accept it as a gift, and, in fact, he visited our church one day. We were actually able to minister to him, and he learned some valuable principles. Eventually, a relationship developed, and we began to see more of him.

One day I had a need, and he was able to help me. For this I not only paid him, but I thought of others who could use his services. I knew many other ministers who needed the same kind of help, and I was able to open doors for the man. This helped him more than he could have dreamed. Today he has a successful business with many employees.

We gave to this man with no expectations of a return. If we had expected a return, we probably would have been offended. But we knew we were following the leading of the Lord by giving him the gift in the first place. Besides, we wanted to help him. When you help someone and open doors for them, and they don't remember to show you gratitude, you must not let what they should or should not do affect you on the inside. God is your Source, and you should always trust in Him.

Chapter 30

Don't Keep Score

The most meaningful aspects of a healthy relationship are that no one keeps score when one person does something for the other. This ensures that there are no demands put on either party. For example, many people regularly keep score of who called whom, or who invited whom to dinner. We frequently hear, "We invited them out last time, so let's wait for them to invite us." Or, "I called them last time; let's wait for them to call us." But I want to propose that love doesn't keep track; it gives.

Keeping score only frustrates those involved in the relationship. The apostle Paul wrote, **Love...seeketh not her own.** Or, as 1 Corinthians 13:5 TLB puts it, **Love does not demand its own way.**

The word *demand* is interesting. It's another form of "to ask"—the kind of asking that leaves no chance of refusal. It reminds me of the spoiled children we sometimes see harassing their parents in grocery stores, crying, "Buy me this. I want that. Yes, you *said I could.* No! I don't want *that;* I want this. Buy it *now.* You *promised!"* Their raucous demands grate on the nerves of the rest of us, quickly driving us away.

Paul points out a gentler, friendlier way:

Love does not demand its own way. It is not irritable or touchy. It does not hold grudges and will hardly even notice when others do it wrong. It is never glad about injustice, but rejoices whenever truth wins out. If you love someone you will be loyal to him no matter what the cost.

1 Corinthians 13:5-7 TLB

I don't see any demanding or keeping count here; I see only giving and understanding.

In his book *The Road Less Traveled*, the psychiatrist Dr. Scott Peck writes,

Whenever we think of ourselves as doing something for someone else, we are in some way denying our own responsibility. Whatever we do is done because we choose to do it, and we make that choice because it is the one that satisfies us the most. Whatever we do for someone else, we do because it fulfills a need we have. Anyone who genuinely loves knows the pleasure of loving. When we genuinely love, we do so because we want to love. We have children because we want to have children, and if we are loving parents, it is because we want to be loving parents. It is true that love involves a change in the self, but this is an extension of the self rather than a sacrifice of the self. Genuine love is a self-replenishing activity. It enlarges rather than diminishes the self; it fills the self rather than depleting it.[1]

Keeping score, or refusing to understand and give, leads to our own frustration. When we do this, we are no longer doing what satisfies us. Both the apostle Paul and Dr. Scott Peck point out that love is about giving. It replenishes and enlarges the giver.

As I look back at some of the significant relationships of my life, I find I've learned that a genuine relationship is built on trust, time and the right motives. Keeping score, which is based on inferior motives, only sabotages all three of these foundations upon which a healthy relationship is built. You should know that if you are the only one doing the giving, then it is not a healthy relationship.

Chapter 31

Control Your Expectations

To prevent ourselves from keeping score, we must first learn not to have unrealistic expectations of others. This practice holds true in relationships as well as in church government. Let me give you an example of what I mean about unrealistic expectations in church government. Pastors tend to expect certain responses from deacons and elders. In turn, deacons and elders have a responsibility to live up to, but they should do so from hearts of servitude toward the Lord.

No matter what our positions in the church—deacon, elder, teacher, children's worker or even pastor—if we find we can no longer live up to our responsibilities, we should go to a supervisor and explain the dilemma.

Let me hasten to say that when anybody takes a position in a church but doesn't fulfill his or her responsibilities, the pastor is forced to take action. You see, there's a trust between a pastor and his staff. Rather than becoming offended when a trust is broken, the two parties should work through their differences. They should find out why a staff member can't live up to his or her responsibilities. For example, there may be adjustments that should be made. Should the church give a little more? Should the staff member give more? Are the rules fair?

If it becomes necessary for the staff member to be relieved of his or her responsibilities, neither side should become offended. If both parties have worked toward solving the problem, then neither side should be upset.

We should deal with our interpersonal expectations in the same way. Ask the tough questions: *Why have I placed an expectation upon this person? Is this expectation realistic? What kind of relationship do we have? Could this relationship be improved if I quit expecting this much?*

It is important to first understand what kind of relationship we're seeking, including which direction we want to take with it. After we've done this, we can confront problem issues with a spirit of love and without anger. I understand that's not always easy, but it's necessary for a successful relationship.

I'm not going to tell you that confronting people is easy or fun. But when two people confront one another in the right spirit, resolving to work through any situation, it can work. It is the responsibility of godly friends to walk in love with each other and to work out their differences.

The Bible teaches that the devil will try to devour us, using all kinds of devices against us. **Be sober, be vigilant; because your adversary the devil, as a roaring lion, walketh about, seeking whom he may devour** (1 Peter 5:8).

Even though we may think our relationships are nearly perfect, we need to watch for attacks from the enemy. If we don't walk in love, we may find somewhere along the line that Satan brings up things to cause division among us. But remember, he can only do it if we allow him to.

One thing I've seen happen over and over between husbands and wives, siblings, and ministers alike is two people expecting something from one another and getting offended when they don't get it. This usually occurs when one person doesn't let the other person know his or her expectations.

Usually someone feels rejected and hurt because expectations weren't fulfilled. Then, perhaps, the other person denies there ever was a need. One of them usually becomes upset, and many times they both walk away offended.

Oftentimes, though, one doesn't even know why the other got hurt. Maybe he recognizes that something is bothering the other person, and he asks if the other is hurt or offended. However, if there is no communication between the two, both parties remain in the dark. This is how strong, negative emotions can enter into a relationship and then lead to irreconcilable differences or retaliation.

For example, suppose that one party in a relationship receives special treatment or privileges from someone else. Now, suppose the time comes for those privileges to cease, and suddenly this person must share those privileges with someone else. It is quite likely that this person will begin to wonder, *What have I done wrong?* The truth is, most likely, nothing. It's just that a change has taken place.

Many times, we are unwilling to accept change. It is not uncommon for us to take things personally, letting the devil drive division between us and our friends. When we let the devil run away with our imaginations and believe his lies, we get into trouble.

When this happens, instead of breaking off a relationship or blaming the other person, practice walking in love and growing through the problem. Even if you were mistreated, you should not take offense, and maybe you will be able to maintain the relationship. Don't allow pride to control you, because if you allow yourself to get offended, you can lose trust in others. Don't allow yourself to become wounded to the point that no real relationship can develop until you get healed.

Take steps to prevent a rift in your friendships. For example, whenever changes are anticipated, communication should be increased so that all parties in a relationship can be prepared. Should someone forget to convey information during a transition, however, remain gracious and exhibit a spirit of patience and understanding.

From time to time, I've failed to fulfill the expectations of people close to me. Perhaps sometimes they have expected too much from me. For example, maybe they have expected me to call them or spend time with them when, in fact, they made no effort to make time or show any interest in getting together. When I've failed to meet others' expectations like that, they've sometimes been offended with me and walked away from the relationships.

Attempting to reconcile with people who harbor offenses can be tricky. Usually, when I call to ask where they've been, they make excuses and say they've been really busy. Invariably, rather than telling me the truth so I could deal with the matter, they offer excuses.

Sometimes church volunteers feel they don't get the recognition or gratitude they deserve. When this happens, they can get hurt or offended and walk away. Indeed, church leaders should appreciate their volunteers, but these people need to ask themselves some questions. Namely, are they serving for selfish reasons? Are they trying to please God or man? Are they serving God with all their hearts and thanking Him for the opportunity to use their gifts and talents to minister to others? Volunteers in the church need to remember to look to God for their reward, not man.

People who serve in leadership in the ministry must ask themselves these same questions. Also, they should add to them the following questions: Am I volunteering only so I can be recognized? Am I trying to gain a place of importance? Am I trying to get close to the pastor? Am I positioning myself in a place to get information? Am I serving only for a paycheck?

Serving in the ministry for any of these reasons is wrong. You should be able to honestly say that your only motive for serving is to minister to God's children. That way, even if you never received any recognition or thanks, you wouldn't get upset, hurt or offended and quit the church and blame everyone else. But if you serve a ministry from a heart of love, you will be able to look into the matter from God's point of view.

Let's look at what the Bible says about this subject.

I therefore...appeal to and beg you to walk (lead a life) worthy of the [divine] calling to which you have been called—with behavior that is a credit to the summons to God's service, living as becomes you— with complete lowliness of mind (humility) and meekness (unselfishness), gentleness, (mildness), with patience, bearing with one another and making allowances because you love one another. Be eager and strive earnestly to guard and keep the harmony and oneness of [produced by] the Spirit in the binding power of peace.

Ephesians 4:1-3 AMP

The world's way of doing business is to expect something in return. God's way is to give unconditionally, without strings attached. God set the example for us when He, out of His great love for us, gave His only Son as the supreme gift. What a gift that was! Not only did God give Jesus, but He also allowed Him to become the sacrifice that would redeem us back to Himself. Having given us His Son, would He withhold anything from us?

We, too, should give out of hearts of love, without expecting a return from people. One way to test our motives for giving is to watch how we act during Christmastime, when the pressure is on to give beyond our means. It is during this time that we often go into debt to meet the expectations of friends and family. Many of us think we cannot eliminate a person from our lists because that person may become hurt if he or she doesn't receive a gift from us. The truth is that we may be holding that person in bondage by our giving.

For example, we may be creating a cycle of giving in which he or she feels compelled to give things to us in return. This should be avoided. We should also not allow people to pressure us to live up to a lifestyle we cannot afford. It is important for us to prevent ourselves from getting under that bondage, particularly during the Christmas season.

Over the years, people have given Sharon and me very nice Christmas gifts that we've truly appreciated. There have been times when a part of me wanted to rush out and buy them something in return, even though I really couldn't afford to do so. Then there were times when we genuinely loved someone and wanted to show our appreciation to him or her. So, out of a pure motive, we would buy an expensive gift on our credit card to show our appreciation. In the months following Christmas, however, as we struggled to pay the credit card bill, we wondered if they even appreciated the gift.

Neither should we become offended with others over other trivial matters. Perhaps we've given someone a present and received nothing in return. Hurt and offended, we fall back on that old saying, "It's not the price or the kind of gift that matters; it's the thought that counts." And yet we think, *Surely he or she could have given me* something *in return*.

I sometimes give things to people who have no need of a gift—they already have everything. But I've discovered that if it is God's will for me to give to someone, He'll give me creative gift ideas for that person. And usually it's something he or she really appreciates.

Again, if we never get anything in return when we give, God always remembers. And He will always provide a harvest for the seed we've sown.

I've learned the hard way that I shouldn't expect too much from people. It's taken a long time, but I've learned that when I give something, I must give it from my heart because I love that person.

Moreover, if I really care about that person, and if he or she fails to respond as I expect, I have to release it to God. That person's response has nothing to do with whether or not I will ever give him or her another gift. That is only determined by my love for the person.

Chapter 32

Dealing With Unfulfilled Expectations

One Sunday afternoon Sharon and I took two of our precious grandchildren on a surprise outing. We were as excited as they were because we love to surprise them.

"First, we're going to have a nice lunch together," I told them, "and then guess what we're going to do?"

Brooke, who was seven at the time, and Chad, who was nine, giggled and played the game, guessing all sorts of things. Finally, I couldn't keep it from them any longer, "Grandma and I are taking you to the circus!"

They got so excited that the circus was all they could talk about during the meal. Sharon and I joined in, building up their expectations. We described the different animals and told them about the various tricks they would do. We talked about tightrope walkers, lion tamers and funny clowns. And, as we described all the fun awaiting us at the circus, their expectations grew.

After lunch, we loaded into the car and headed for the circus. At their insistence, we described the animals again, one by one, as they showered us with hugs and kisses. Brooke couldn't wait to get inside and buy a Coke and some popcorn. It was such a happy time that even the traffic could not squelch their enthusiasm.

I remembered that I didn't have much money in my pocket, but I knew Sharon always had money. So I thought, *Why sweat it?* But as we waited in line to get our tickets, we discovered a small problem—Sharon didn't have much money with her either. *Oh, well,* I thought, *I know they will take a credit card.* So when it was our turn, I presented my credit card to the clerk.

"Oh, we don't accept credit cards, sir," the lady at the booth said, "but inside the doors we have an ATM where you can use your credit card to get some cash."

Sharon and I looked at each other with blank expressions; neither of us knew the code to get our money from the ATM. We'd never used the credit card that way before. All at once the children began to realize what was going on. Their excitement was turning to disappointment. Meanwhile, I was trying to do everything I could to make this work out.

We walked around outside the circus for a while, trying to figure out what to do. It was getting near show time, so there was no time to run home for money. There was just nothing we could do. Brooke's and Chad's little faces looked up at us, heavy with disappointment. Tears began streaming down Brooke's face.

"Papa, you promised!"

It hurt me to see her upset like that, because I had raised her expectations so high and now I couldn't fulfill my promise to her. I tried to appease her. I took her to the place where many of the animals were kept between shows, but nothing would suffice. She wanted to go inside to see the circus. Since we couldn't make it happen, there was nothing else to do but go home.

Back in the car with two completely unhappy children, I promised to take them again. But their hearts were set on going that day—not sometime in the future. Before long, I was able to comfort Chad and convince him that we would go back soon. Brooke, on the other hand, took longer to convince. I had to earn back her trust.

Within a few hours, my grandchildren had experienced exhilarating expectations followed by a devastating disappointment. We made it up to them another day, however, by taking them to the circus after all. But this time they reminded us to take money before we left the house!

How many times have you been hurt because someone raised your expectations and then did not fulfill them? Perhaps you experienced a letdown in childhood like my grandchildren did. Maybe your parents promised to bring you a present but for some reason they forgot. Or, as an adult, maybe a spouse promised to take you on an exciting vacation that never happened. Perhaps a boss promised you a promotion that never came through. Any of these unfulfilled expectations can leave you disheartened and disappointed.

To some people, disappointment can be devastating, while to others, it's just a part of life. Of course, your reaction to disappointment will depend on your level of expectation. However, the truth is that you don't have to live with disappointment. You have a choice, a way to escape the disappointment of unmet expectations.

Of course, the best way to avoid them is to avoid them in the first place. I want to help you avoid potential situations that produce unfulfilled expectations. For example, never expect something from someone before you've told that person what you expect. Otherwise, you're sure to be disappointed. By not communicating your needs, you set yourself up to be disappointed.

Perhaps you've even experienced unfulfilled expectations in your prayer life. If so, you're not alone. Many born-again, Spirit-filled Christians struggle with this issue. I've talked with countless people who have prayed for things they did not get right away. And when they did not see immediate results or receive results exactly the way they wanted, they grew angry with God and started murmuring or complaining.

You need to know that God is a good God and He will never hurt you. He is not the God of disappointment but of fulfillment. God has never let anybody down, and He won't let you down either.

Chapter 33

Risk Friendship

Sometimes being a good friend involves taking risks. If you aren't willing to go out on a limb once in a while to pursue a relationship, you probably won't have many friends. You see, friendship is a privilege, an opportunity for personal growth and sometimes even a risk, but it should never be an obligation. If you want more friends, you might have to take a risk to find them.

Yes, it's true. Risking friendship involves becoming vulnerable to someone. You may risk being hurt, sometimes even deeply, when you become involved in a relationship. But friendship is such a priceless gift that I recommend you take the risk. The rewards of a good friendship far outweigh the risk.

Actually, most successful relationships don't come together because the two people involved planned for them to come together. I believe God brings about successful, divine relationships. It pays to take the risk of entering into friendships.

PART VII

Guard Your Emotions

Chapter 34

Submit Your
Emotions to God

It's really important for us to understand how to take care of our emotions. Our emotions are those feelings, both positive and negative, that provide so much meaning, and sometimes pain, to our lives. Our emotions can enrich our lives, but controlling them is key.

I once overheard an argument between a boy and girl. She was really nagging him about something he had done that could not be fixed or changed. He hadn't done anything to hurt her; rather, he had done something that only hurt himself.

Because of the anger and pain I saw on their faces, I intervened and tried to help. I approached the girl, saying, "You know, he can't change what has happened. Therefore, the only thing to do is forgive him for what's already been done. Besides, if what he did doesn't affect you, you shouldn't be so upset about it."

Fortunately, she was able to back away and look at the situation with some objectivity. She was able to detach from her emotions, and her perspective changed. Thus, her nagging ceased.

By learning to change our perspective and refusing to concentrate on the problems, we can better control our emotions and tendency to nag. By the way, the word "nag" comes from the Old

Norse word *gnaga* and the Old English word *gnagan*, both of which mean "to gnaw." Today, it has come to mean "to find fault or complain incessantly."

Too often we become upset about something and gnaw at it as dogs gnaw at bones. We need to avoid behaving like animals, grumbling and murmuring, growling and snarling, until we make ourselves and our friends sick.

The Bible talks about what happens when people complain. David said, **I complained, and my spirit was overwhelmed** (Ps. 77:3). The apostle Paul said the children of Israel were destroyed in the wilderness because they murmured continually. That's why God commands us not to murmur. (1 Cor. 10:10.) Not only is murmuring disastrous to relationships, but it also appears to be hazardous to our health!

Proverbs 4:23 says, "Watch over your heart with all diligence, for from it flow the springs of life." This Scripture warns us to guard our emotions. Once unbridled, negative emotions can overcome us and ruin our relationships. But we don't have to let that happen. And the best way I've discovered to prevent that is to control our emotions by submitting them to God.

Submitting your emotions to God really works. As time goes on, I've noticed my relationship with Sharon getting better and better. Because we work at being together peacefully, we enjoy spending time together. Furthermore, when one of us makes a mistake or does something that might have hurt the other, we don't keep driving that negative point home. We leave it and go on, because we know we must forgive and overlook one another's faults in order to move on. We've discovered that as we submit our emotions to God, He changes us and helps us to see things from His viewpoint.

There are times, however, when instead of submitting their emotions to God, some people lose control and break up good relationships. For example, let's say one person gets mad at another person for revealing a very personal secret between the two of them. Then, if the other person gets offended and retaliates by exposing things that were also said in confidence, just to get even, that person damages the relationship.

When secrets are leaked and information is distorted to make another person look bad, trust is violated. Getting offended and betraying someone's confidence is wrong. Decisions based on bitterness are never good, because they dig a deeper pit for the embittered person.

Usually what happens is that the other person begins to fight back and defend himself or try to get even. He begins to tell his side, emotionally, and sometimes with wrong motives. Very often, he begins to reveal things that were told to him in confidence, because he knows it will hurt the other person. This starts a vicious cycle, and the battle rages on and on. After a while, both parties can fall away from God and become tormented by unforgiveness.

This is why we should turn to God, submit our emotions to Him and let Him restore us. As we submit our emotions to God and forgive the ones who have hurt us, we become free inside. Then we can take this freedom and ask those people to forgive us. Our joy will return, and a spirit of victory will begin to allow us to form new relationships and strengthen existing ones.

I know this is true because it has happened to me.

In the 70s, a close friend and I had grown to really trust each other—or at least I thought we had. We had worked together for nearly ten years when I began to notice a change in his life and his doctrine. We stopped spending as much time together, and when we did get together, we seemed to have nothing in common anymore. I didn't know what to do. I would try to talk to him, but I just couldn't seem to get anywhere.

After a while, I began hearing things about him that I didn't believe or didn't want to believe. So one day I approached him about them. I asked him if the things I had been hearing were true, and he blew up at me. He denied everything.

If he was doing something wrong, I didn't want to judge him. I only wanted to help. But he chose, instead, to reject my sincerity. Being young and inexperienced, I got hurt.

In our last scheduled meeting together, he attacked me and put me down from the pulpit. That really hurt, and I found myself dealing with it in an immature manner. At first, I tried to go on as though it were not happening, but it got worse. In some other meetings, he slandered me. I didn't handle this well, either. I got into the feud he had started and began to privately reveal his confirmed sin. My excuse for doing this was that he was hurting me publicly, so I felt it was my duty to let people know he was deceiving them. In truth, I was hurt, offended and felt like I had to defend myself. I was trying to get even with him. And the more he would talk about me, the more I would talk about his sin to others privately.

But God says, **Let no corrupt communication proceed out of your mouth, but that which is good to the use of edifying, that it may minister grace unto the hearers** (Eph. 4:29). Furthermore, **But now ye also put off all these; anger, wrath, malice, blasphemy, filthy communication out of your mouth** (Col. 3:8).

Unfortunately, I was blinded by the whole thing and didn't particularly want to hear what God had to say. Anger and bitterness kept me from focusing on my calling and mission in life. And the damage I caused myself as a result took its toll. I began to pray to get over this, speaking to "this mountain" to move. I quoted the following over and over, many times a day.

> **For verily I say unto you, That whosoever shall say unto this mountain, Be thou removed, and be thou cast into the sea; and shall not doubt in his heart, but shall believe that those things which he saith shall come to pass; he shall have whatsoever he saith.**
>
> **Mark 11:24**

As I did this, the Lord began to deal with me about Mark 11:25. That passage says, **And when ye stand praying, forgive, if ye have aught against any: that your Father also which is in heaven may forgive you your trespasses.**

I realized I had been wrong. I tried unsuccessfully to reach the minister to make an appointment to ask him to forgive me. I even went to a few of his meetings, hoping to have the opportunity to talk with him, but I was unable to reach him. Eventually, I just forgave him and put it behind me.

God restored me, and in the process I learned two great lessons: (1) We can't get even, and (2) we shouldn't talk about others' failures. When we violate these two principles, we only hurt ourselves and get caught up in a terrible web that winds tighter and tighter until our spiritual lives suffer.

Many years had passed since I'd seen this minister. Then one day I heard he was coming to town, so I decided to attend his meeting. After seeing him, I could tell he was still suffering as a result of unforgiveness. The attendance at his meeting was small, and his attitude was bad. It was obvious that he was still blaming me and others for his problems.

After the meeting, I approached him, and, to my surprise, he did talk to me. He even asked me to go to lunch. At lunch, our conversation consisted primarily of small talk, but I found I could look at him without bitterness or resentment. Because I had totally forgiven him many years ago, I was free to enjoy his company. He, on the other hand, was still in bondage to his bitterness, and he visibly lacked the joy I had been blessed with.

By working through this experience and others like it through the years, I've come to appreciate the wisdom of Romans 13:8 more and more. That Scripture says, **Owe no man anything, but to love one another.** Loving one another is not burdensome when God's Word is deep inside of your heart.

First John 4:18 describes the beauty of godly love: **There is no fear in love; but perfect love casteth out fear: because fear hath torment. He that feareth is not made perfect in love.**

The beauty of godly love is that as we grow up and mature in it, we can enjoy a better quality of life. When we walk in love, we don't need to criticize, fear or be jealous of another person's success anymore. With God's love, we can enjoy success inside of us that will ultimately work its way out.

This success begins in our individual relationships with God. Time spent in prayer, talking to Him about our emotional responses to others, will first of all calm us down and help us to become more objective. Second, as we submit to God, He will guide and instruct us on how to properly respond to other people. And after we begin improving our responses to others, we become a "threefold cord," a relationship team, which is not easily broken" (Eccl. 4:12).

Chapter 35

Don't Let Friends Upset You

No matter where you are—at home, on the job, at church or on vacation—there will invariably be people who will take delight in upsetting you. Some will harass, pick on, criticize, make fun of, torment or do whatever it takes to get a negative response from you. Those kinds of people enjoy seeing others upset; they enjoy breaking up relationships; and they enjoy getting people off course in life. Proverbs 16:28 talks about these types: **A froward man soweth strife: and a whisperer separateth chief friends.**

As you know, we've been talking about guarding our emotions. Now let's talk about learning how not to upset our friends. Jesus knew there would be people who would make it their mission in life to upset and distract believers. But, interestingly, Jesus didn't address those people. He said, "Anyone who lets himself be distracted from the work I plan for him is not fit for the kingdom of God." (Luke 9:62.)

God has a plan for our lives, and that plan includes protection against our enemies. Included in that plan may be certain jobs, relationships, church fellowship and other wonderful things that He doesn't want us to miss out on. Therefore, it's important that we guard ourselves from offenses that would come along and cause us to respond rashly. God's plan for our lives is too important for us to just ruin it by allowing another person's actions to open a way for the devil to gain a foothold in our lives.

Instead of getting upset and responding emotionally, we should keep our eyes on God and seek His peace in all circumstances. That's why Isaiah said God would keep us in perfect peace if we would keep our minds on Him. (Isa. 26:3.) And Jesus said, **In me ye...have peace** (John 16:33).

"If peace be in the heart," wrote Charles Francis Richardson, "the wildest winter storm is full of solemn beauty, the midnight flash but shows the path of duty, each living creature tells some new and joyous story, the very trees and stones all catch a ray of glory, if peace be in the heart."

Chapter 36

Respond in Love; Don't React in Anger

People often say and do hurtful things to one another. When people treat us this way, we must respond with love rather than reacting in anger. The apostle Paul apparently experienced the same problem. He wrote in Galatians 2:20, **I am crucified with Christ: nevertheless I live; yet not I, but Christ liveth in me: and the life which I now live in the flesh I live by the faith of the Son of God, who loved me, and gave himself for me.** He also wrote, **I die daily** (1 Cor. 15:31), meaning that every day he crucified his selfish ambitions.

Dying daily to our selfish ambitions and feelings is one way to avoid reacting emotionally to adverse circumstances. Many times I've found myself in these kinds of hurtful situations. That's why I start each day in prayer, bringing my flesh under subjection. That's also why I sometimes slip away during the day and talk to God, saying, "God, stand up on the inside of me. Don't let my thoughts and emotions control me now; I want the Spirit of God to control me."

Another way to prevent an emotional reaction is to exercise our power of choice. We can choose to control our emotions and follow the "ten be's" for lasting friendships.[1] Do you know what the "ten be's" for lasting relationships are? In case you don't, I'll list them below.

Right and Wrong Expectations in Friendship

1. **Be interested.** By showing an interest in others' interests, you transfer attention from feelings to actions or thoughts. This diffuses negative emotions on both sides.

2. **Be unselfish.** By taking the initiative and doing things for the other person and by giving more than your friend expects, you again transfer attention from the potentially volatile to the neutral emotional response level. This should provide for an unemotional response in most cases.

3. **Be thoughtful.** Show others how much you appreciate them by bringing cheer into their lives. By doing this, they will find it more difficult to lose their tempers with you because you have established up front that you truly care about them. Then, any minor disagreements become just that—minor disagreements. (A word of caution here: Avoid saying, "How can you react this way after all I have done for you?" That statement will be like pouring gasoline on a raging fire!)

4. **Be considerate.** Make it a habit to listen carefully to the ideas and opinions of others without responding rashly, even when those ideas or opinions may seem trivial, unimportant or downright ridiculous. Never forget that your friends' ideas may be their seriously held convictions. Laughing at or arguing over these ideas may breed dissension, anger and hostility.

5. **Be true.** Loyalty and fidelity are the highest compliments you can give your friends. Being loyal implies being faithful and steadfast in the face of any temptation that may threaten you to renounce, desert or betray a friendship. The word "fidelity" implies a strict and continuing faithfulness to an obligation, trust or duty.

Lasting relationships are based on trust; and trust, I have observed, is exchanged for both loyalty and fidelity. It is that sense of well-being and safety that comes from knowing your friend is faithful to you no matter what trouble may come your way. It's hard to be angry with someone who loves you no matter what happens. (That's why most of us have pets— they give us the faithfulness our friends usually won't!)

6. **Be cheerful and optimistic.** Your friends usually have all the trouble they can handle already without taking on your problems too. People who carry more than one load of responsibility can become irritable and quarrelsome very quickly. The good news is that you can diffuse much of this ugliness by being upbeat and optimistic and by leaving your gloom behind.

7. **Be dependable.** When you let someone down, break a promise or go back on your word for whatever reason, you discredit that person and undermine your relationship with him or her. A Christian should be as good as his word, whether or not there is a written contract. A friend should be even better. (A word of caution: Obviously, true emergencies sometimes do interfere with even the best plans. When that happens, you should explain it to your friend honestly. An honest explanation given at the earliest possible moment usually diffuses anger.)

8. **Be confident.** Your friends need you to show the same faith in their abilities that you show in your own. They want you to avoid making a comparison between yourself and them or between your choices and theirs. For example, I know two women who share fairly equal abilities, talents and incomes. They also seem to be good friends on the surface, but one of them is continually involved in "one-upmanship." For

instance, if the first woman gets a new car, the second woman has to buy a newer, more expensive car.

This kind of competitiveness can exist for a while, but eventually, if not checked, it will lead to anger, resentment, bitterness, altercations and finally a break in the relationship. The best way to avoid such emotional reactions as these is to accept your friends for who they are and refuse to compare yourself to them.

9. **Be helpful.** Friends help each other—without charge. Negative emotional reactions are triggered when helping becomes "being taken advantage of" and when "need" becomes "freeloading." A good rule of thumb to remember in situations like these is to quickly return a friend's favor in kind. For example, if your friend freely helps you build a deck in your backyard, offer to help with one of his projects. If you cannot find an "in-kind favor" to perform, then do something else special that you know your friend would like. It need not be expensive, but it should be especially tailored to your friend's interests.

10. **Be courteous.** "Without doubt," writes L.J. DuBois in *Life's Intimate Friendships,* "one of the greatest barriers to friendship, is the 'loud-mouthed,' insincere, overbearing, meddling, ungracious spirit which rides roughshod over the rights and feelings of others." How unfortunate it is that we so often tend to treat friends and family with great discourtesy. These should be the most important people to us on earth. They are the ones for whom our courtesy should be most genuine. It is amazing how much anger genuine courtesy can diffuse.

These are the "ten be's" of friendship. Remember, you always have a choice. Each and every day, you have a choice. You may not be able to choose how somebody treats you, but you can choose how to respond.

Sadly, however, many of us live as though life just happens to us—like victims—when, in actuality, we can avoid choosing substandard, leftover, undesirable and messed-up lives. (You can learn more about how to do this in my book, *Never Be a Victim Again*.) God has so much more for us, but we must be convinced that it's ours before we can partake of it. That's simply the truth. When we acknowledge the good things God has provided for us, we can choose victory.

Chapter 37

Give No Place to the Devil

While it is true that we do have choices in our relationships, we must be careful to make the right ones according to what we know from the Word. Making wrong choices may be giving the devil a place in our lives.

For example, we're giving him a place when we look for ways to justify wrong actions. We have to be careful when we hear ourselves sounding overly defensive.

If you're right and everybody else is wrong too often, you'd better examine yourself. For example, you might think you should leave a church just because they're not preaching what you think they should. Well, that's giving place to the devil. When you think everyone is against you or you change your relationships like you change clothes, something is wrong.

God laid out a pattern of behavior for Christians to follow that prevents the devil from gaining a foothold in our lives and relationships. Let's look at Ephesians 4:17-32 TLB:

> Let me say this, then, speaking for the Lord: Live no longer as the unsaved do, for they are blinded and confused. Their closed hearts are full of darkness; they are far away from the life of God because they have shut their minds against him, and they cannot

understand his ways. They don't care anymore about right and wrong and have given themselves over to impure ways. They stop at nothing, being driven by their evil minds and reckless lusts.

But that isn't the way Christ taught you! If you have really heard his voice and learned from him the truths concerning himself, then throw off your old evil nature—the old you that was a partner in your evil ways—rotten through and through, full of lust and shame.

Now your attitudes and thoughts must all be constantly changing for the better. Yes, you must be a new and different person, holy and good. Clothe yourself with this new nature.

Stop lying to each other; tell the truth, for we are parts of each other and when we lie to each other we are hurting ourselves. If you are angry, don't sin by nursing your grudge. Don't let the sun go down with you still angry—get over it quickly; for when you are angry you give a mighty foothold to the devil.

If anyone is stealing he must stop it and begin using those hands of his for honest work so he can give to others in need. Don't use bad language. Say only what is good and helpful to those you are talking to, and what will give them a blessing.

Don't cause the Holy Spirit sorrow by the way you live. Remember, he is the one who marks you to be present on that day when salvation from sin will be complete.

Stop being mean, bad-tempered and angry. Quarreling, harsh words, and dislike of others should have no place in your lives. Instead, be kind to each other, tenderhearted, forgiving one another, just as God has forgiven you because you belong to Christ.

This lends further insight to God's command that you "Watch over your heart with all diligence, for from it flow the springs of life." (Prov. 4:23.) Left unguarded, negative emotions can control and ruin otherwise good relationships. But you don't have to let that happen. God has provided a way of escape. All you have to do is submit your emotions to Him, and He will show you how to fix the problem and move on to victory.

Chapter 38

Insecure People Treat You the Way They See Themselves

We've all had to deal with insecure people—those whose moods sometimes seem unreasonable, illogical and uncaring. Insecure people sometimes insist they're right when it's blatantly obvious they're wrong. Other times, they worry about problems that do not even exist. Additionally, other insecure people refuse to make decisions, become afraid for no reason, buckle under criticism or even become depressed for seemingly no reason.

All of these symptoms can possibly point to one problem. And usually the problem insecure people face is simply this: Feelings of insecurity have overwhelmed their feelings of confidence. They find themselves caught in a whirlwind of dark emotions as though they're caught in a vortex where they grab at anything for safety and stability. Their feelings of insecurity can overwhelm and even emotionally incapacitate them.

Insecure people are often unsure of themselves and of how to behave around others. Perhaps some of them will admit there is a problem—that their moods are unreasonable, illogical and insensitive toward others—but the truth is that most insecure people find it difficult to break patterns of negative behavior. This usually happens because this behavior has worked for them in the past and has become a habit. (And we all know how hard it is to break habits.)

Now, let me say this. I realize we *all* have some areas in which we feel insecure. That's normal. The kind of insecurity I'm talking about is the kind that debilitates a person.

When someone is that insecure, they usually cause others to suffer as a result of their insecurity. They may look healthy, but often they are carrying around deep wounds, hurts and pain that demand attention.

If this problem isn't fixed, insecure people can pass their insecurity from one generation to the next, unconsciously perpetuating that debilitating force. I'm not a psychologist, and I don't claim to know all the causes behind feelings of insecurity, but I do know God can transform an insecure individual into a glowing, whole and healthy person if he or she will ask Him to. It may involve working at it diligently with God's Word to overcome these feelings, but it can happen.

In the book *Introduction to Psychology & Counseling,* authors Meier, Minirth and Wichern state, "Total health in a whole person demands healthy relationships in three areas—inward toward self, outward toward others, and upward toward God."[1] To achieve this state of health, one must be at peace and cultivate a good relationship with himself, with others and with God.

To be emotionally healthy means to be at peace. Even secure people may be at peace in just one or two of these areas (inward toward self, outward toward others and upward toward God), but perhaps not in all three.

I want to share with you ten characteristics of a secure person, with the hope that you will become aware of what it means to be secure. For each characteristic, I will also list some signs of insecurity. If you find any of these indicators in your own life, it's a sure signal that you need to submit that aspect of your life to God, asking for His help in that area.

The First Characteristic of a Secure Person

The secure person functions normally physically, emotionally and intellectually. Not only does the secure person function normally with these qualities, but he or she is balanced in these areas.[2] The secure person is not afraid to use his or her mind to feel and express emotions. Likewise, the secure person is not ashamed of his or her body. The secure person regards these aspects of life as being acceptable and functional without too much thought. Whereas the insecure person is plagued by worry, anxiety and depression, the secure person is able to function normally without these problems.

The Second Characteristic of a Secure Person

The secure person adapts to change, using self-control and discipline.[3] The secure person deals with stress and change effectively.

Let me tell you what I mean by this. Suppose somebody you know has been laid off from his job. If he were a secure person, he would go out and attempt to get another job as quickly as possible, start a business or make other arrangements to cover his family's needs despite any feelings of anxiety. The insecure person, on the other hand, may delay this duty, indulging instead in a pity party, while denying that anything is wrong.

The Third Characteristic of a Secure Person

The secure person maintains an attitude of confidence and optimism, which is usually accompanied by a sense of humor.[4]

Such a person believes first in God's provision and then in his or her own ability to make competent decisions. On the other hand, the insecure person wanders around in indecision and uncertainty, perpetually reluctant to make decisions.

The Fourth Characteristic of a Secure Person

The secure person exhibits an unwavering sense of purpose for life, undergirded by meritorious goals and an eternal perspective.[5] There is something about having an eternal perspective that focuses one's life very quickly.

It's very difficult for a believer to be concerned with petty, selfish things when he or she has an eternal perspective. I've also discovered that those who set goals and move toward them resolutely aren't usually disconcerted or easily thwarted by life's distractions.

On the other hand, the insecure person lacks goals or direction and lets life push him or her around. Therefore, it's not surprising that when relationship problems occur, the insecure person allows him- or herself to be pushed around in that area too.

The Fifth Characteristic of a Secure Person

The secure person relates well to a variety of people.[6] Position or fame does not particularly impress such a person. Neither does a person's income or education level intimidate a secure person. The secure person has a strong sense of self and portrays the real person, regardless of who is around. Because of this, he or she also performs well on the job, makes and keeps friends and loves and accepts love in return.

Meier, Minirth and Wichern recognize "a capacity for intimacy in close interpersonal relationships as a clue to mental health."[7] Conversely, feelings of insecurity may hamper a person's job performance, relationships and capacity to love, leaving the person angry, frustrated and embittered.

The Sixth Characteristic of a Secure Person

The secure person maintains a balance in all areas of his or her life.[8] This means the secure person can either follow or lead without difficulty. Furthermore, such a person equally maintains healthy levels of dependence and independence, while concurrently sustaining a realistic view of self.

The secure person doesn't lock him—or herself into a mold and is not afraid to do things differently. For example, the secure person doesn't need to be in the spotlight all the time, and is not afraid to compromise.

Most importantly, the secure person is balanced spiritually. He or she takes time to read the Word of God, to pray, to witness and to enjoy Christian fellowship—no one aspect is emphasized to the exclusion or diminution of others.

The Seventh Characteristic of a Secure Person

A secure person is dependable.[9] Such a person has developed strong internal standards and is extremely trustworthy. On the other hand, the insecure person seems to be unable to resist social pressures and responds impulsively to the moment.

The Eighth Characteristic of a Secure Person

The secure person is others-centered rather than self-centered.[10] Such a person has enough emotional strength to give to others and still deal with his or her own problems. The secure person can express and control his or her own emotions, does not avoid situations that arouse strong emotions and does not escape into isolation or dissociation. While the secure person accepts any emotion as a potential strength, the insecure person may become wrapped up in darker emotions, such as selfish desire, anger, jealousy and suspicion.

The Ninth Characteristic of a Secure Person

The secure woman is satisfied with her femaleness, and the secure man is satisfied with his maleness.[11] Despite the pressures of changing social attitudes, truly secure people are satisfied with being who they are sexually. They are free from fear regarding sexuality.

The Tenth Characteristic of a Secure Person

The secure person maintains a positive relationship with the Lord.[12] I've found it particularly interesting that generally a secure person is one who daily reads the Bible. It's as though the secure person knows instinctively that God's Word produces peace, joy, contentment and extreme courage. Because of the nurturing one receives from the Bible, the secure person has a rock-like stability that no storm of life can shake.

Over and over again, the Bible addresses the problems and emotions associated with insecurity: **Be anxious for nothing** (Matt. 6:25-34). **Fear thou not; for I am with thee** (Isa. 41:10). **Be not dismayed** (1 Chron. 28:20). **Thou, 0 Lord, art a shield for me** (Ps. 3:3). **Because he is at my right hand, I shall not be moved** (Ps. 16:8). **Fret not. Trust in the Lord. Delight thyself** also in the Lord. **Commit thy way unto the Lord. Rest in the Lord, and wait patiently for him** (Ps. 37:1,3,4,5,7).

God desires for us to be safe and happy. He does not want us to be fraught with fears, anxieties and dark emotions. If we find ourselves plagued with insecurities, we should ask God to remove those things that hinder us from being free.

Chapter 39

Hurting
People
Hurt People

According to an old story, a gentleman walking in a park noticed a young boy sitting on a bench. Concerned by the look on the youth's face, the gentleman asked, "Are you all right?"

"Well, sir, I am in quite a bit of pain," the boy answered.

"What's wrong? Is there something I can do to help?" the man asked.

"Well, I'm sitting on a bumblebee."

"Then why don't you get up?"

"Because I figure right now I'm hurting him more than he's hurting me," the boy replied.

Many people who are in relationships that have gone bad are doing the same thing—trying to get even with those who they perceive have hurt them. They do this despite the fact that getting even requires depriving themselves in some way and treating others poorly.

One day as I was getting my hair cut, I was making conversation with the hairdresser. I asked if she was married.

"I'm divorced," she replied angrily. "I have two children, and that dirty scoundrel left me and our children for another woman!"

Realizing I had asked the wrong question, I tried to help her release some of the bitterness. "Why don't you forgive him and move on with your life?" I asked.

I thought she was going to cut off my ear after that question.

"*Forgive* him! Why should *I* forgive *him? I* didn't do anything. *He* is the one who left me with these children to raise. *I* have to get up and go to work while *he* is out having a good time. I hate this job, so I spend the whole day, every day, thinking of ways I can hurt him and get even with him."

Even though her life was difficult, her hatred and bitterness only made it worse. Miserable and unhappy, she was wasting her life and could not be the best parent for her children because she would not forgive.

God commands us, **This book of the law shall not depart out of thy mouth; but thou shalt meditate therein day and night, that thou mayest observe to do according to all that is written therein: for then thou shalt make thy way prosperous, and then thou shalt have good success** (Josh. 1:8). God said this because He knows that unforgiveness keeps us in bondage, thereby blocking creativity and causing us to be unhappy. It fosters strife and self-pity as well as destructive and wrong attitudes, all of which keep us from living a good life. God's solution to getting rid of unforgiveness is for us to meditate on His Word and obey it.

Sadly, many people watch life pass by, much as the oyster does. The oyster, which has a hard shell, cannot go after anything; it must wait until something comes near it. When people are hurting, they tend to develop hard shells like the oyster's, and they find themselves incapable of letting go of the hurt so they can pursue a better life.

Pursuing Worthless Issues

Some people let unimportant issues become more important to them than good relationships. For several years, I myself allowed unimportant things to distance me from my precious mother. She was a very strict Pentecostal woman with a deep commitment to God, and she had some strong beliefs about certain things that I felt were unimportant, old-fashioned and unscriptural. Each time we were together, she would bring up one of those issues. I would listen, then vigorously state my opinion, backed by a few Scriptures supporting my belief. Even though I knew she would never change her beliefs, I couldn't help arguing with her. I kept trying to change her mind.

She wasn't hurting anyone by what she believed. Besides, she was a godly, wonderful person who was deeply committed to prayer. Often she prayed several hours a day. Sometimes she would pray with a friend on the telephone for an hour or more at a time.

However, I overlooked these qualities for a long time. I allowed our differences to keep us apart for several years, until one day the Lord spoke to me. As I prayed for my mother that time, the Lord instructed me to love her. I was shocked because I thought I did love my mother—I just disagreed with her doctrine.

Of course I loved my mother—I bought her gifts, took her out to eat, invited her over to my house for Christmas and Thanksgiving. We were actually very close. Despite our closeness, however, our times together were unpleasant. Nevertheless, I reminded the Lord of all the things I did for my mother that demonstrated my love for her.

Again, He instructed me to love her.

"I do love her," I replied.

Then God reminded me of 1 Corinthians 13:4-8 TLB:

> **Love is very patient and kind, never jealous or envious, never boastful or proud, never haughty or selfish or rude. Love does not demand its own way. It is not irritable or touchy. It does not hold grudges and will hardly even notice when others do it wrong. It is never glad about injustice, but rejoices whenever the truth wins out. If you love someone you will be loyal to him no matter what the cost. You will always believe in him, always expect the best of him, and always stand your ground in defending him.**
>
> **All the special gifts and powers from God will someday come to an end, but love goes on forever.**

God showed me that what I really thought of my mother was reflected by the way I treated her. And He helped me understand how I could change things if I would focus on loving my mother instead of trying to change her beliefs.

Mother attended a small Pentecostal church that had strict beliefs about what it meant to be godly and what it meant to be worldly. This teaching influenced her commitment to God. And changing those beliefs, in her mind, probably equated to lessening her commitment to God. Needless to say, she was determined not to turn away from God.

I began to understand that by arguing with her, I was keeping us from enjoying each other. So I resolved to avoid any subject of contention between us. If she brought up a touchy topic, I changed the subject and told her instead what a wonderful mother she was and how much I loved her. After doing this for a while, I saw Mother begin to change too. She didn't change her beliefs, but she changed her attitude about our relationship. She knew that our love was stronger than our disagreements. Furthermore, she began to enjoy visiting our church, whereas before she had concentrated only on the issues that separated us.

My attitude also changed. More and more I began to remember all the nice things she had done for me. And as these memories returned, my perspective changed too.

During the last years of her life, we enjoyed a wonderful relationship. Finally, I had quit trying to make her see things my way; instead, I loved her simply for who she was, and that was all that mattered.

We're all tempted to argue with family members or good friends over trivial matters. I remember one day Sharon and I went out to do some important shopping. Along the way, I noticed a particular store and pointed it out to her, saying, "We've never shopped there. We should go there someday."

"Don, you've been in that store," she said.

"I have not been in that store."

"Yes, you have," she shot back.

The day was not getting started very well; I could feel the air in the car getting heavier. I thought about it for a minute, and I found myself really wanting to be right. I wanted to come back with a few choice statements, proving that she was wrong. However, after thinking about it, I realized this was an unimportant issue. It was one of those issues about which I could not change her mind, nor could she change mine. Since it really didn't matter who was right, I dropped the subject and started talking about something else. Sharon really believed she had been in that store with me, and she still does. And I still believe I've never been in that store.

Now and then we bring it up again and laugh about it. It's become a little joke between us, and now we're able to talk about it without caring who is right.

The secret to getting along, I've discovered, is to drop worthless issues that can only lead to confusion, arguments and strife. Paul said it best: **Don't quarrel with anyone. Be at peace with everyone, just as much as possible** (Rom. 12:18 TLB). Paul also instructed his son in the Lord, Timothy:

> **Remind your people of these great facts, and command them in the name of the Lord not to argue over unimportant things. Such arguments are confusing and useless, and even harmful. Work hard so God can say to you, "Well done." Be a good workman, one who does not need to be ashamed when God examines your work. Know what his Word says and means. Steer clear of foolish discussions which lead people into the sin of anger with each other. Things will be said that will burn and hurt for a long time to come.**
>
> 2 Timothy 2:14-17

Chapter 40

Overlook Faults

Seldom is there any value in pointing out another person's faults. Generally, people are aware of their own faults and have already decided whether or not they will do anything about them. None of us can change another person. That person must desire to change himself before any change can come. It is, therefore, important for us to learn to accept and overlook the faults of others. For example, we can try to overlook a friend's knack for being habitually late, or another friend's difficulty in making simple decisions, such as choosing a good restaurant.

God's Word teaches that we must deal with all people patiently, with kindness and longsuffering. That's how God responds to each of us. In fact, let's look more closely at some of the words the Bible uses to describe God's love for us. Four Greek words draw vivid pictures for us throughout the Scriptures: *anecho*, *epieikeia*, *makrothumia* and *hupomone*.

The first word, *anecho*, means "to hold up or hold back" and is translated as "forbearing or forbearance." The translation of the word *epieikeia* is not often used today outside the church; it means "intensely reasonable" and is often translated as meaning "forbearance" or "gentleness." The Greek word *makrothumia* denotes "longsuffering or patience in regard to antagonistic persons." The last Greek word we listed is *hupomone*, which expresses "patience with regard to adverse things."[1]

As you can see, a closer look at these Greek words reveals God's longsuffering and forbearance toward humankind, both saved and unsaved. This gives us an idea of His great love for us. Don't you think that, as children of God, we too should possess that kind of love for others? Yes, all of us share in the human condition and should be honored despite our shortcomings.

Let's go over a few Scriptures regarding faults or weaknesses in others:

> We then that are strong ought to bear the infirmities of the weak, and not to please ourselves.
>
> **Romans 15:1**

> Now we exhort you, brethren, warn them that are unruly, comfort the feebleminded, support the weak, be patient toward all men.
>
> **1 Thessalonians 5:14**

> I therefore, the prisoner for the Lord, appeal to and beg you to walk (lead a life) worthy of the [divine] calling to which you have been called—with behavior that is a credit to the summons to God's service, living as becomes you—with complete lowliness of mind (humility) and meekness (unselfishness, gentleness, mildness), with patience, bearing with one another and making allowances because you love one another.
>
> Be eager and strive earnestly to guard and keep the harmony and oneness of [produced by] the Spirit in the binding power of peace.
>
> **Ephesians 4:1-3** AMP

Since you have been chosen by God who has given you this new kind of life, and because of his deep love and concern for you, you should practice tenderhearted mercy and kindness to others. Don't worry about making a good impression on them but be ready to suffer quietly and patiently. Be gentle and ready to forgive; never hold grudges. Remember, the Lord forgave you, so you must forgive others.

Most of all, let love guide your life, for then the whole church will stay together in perfect harmony.

Colossians 3:12-14 TLB

By looking at these Scriptures, we can clearly see what our instructions are: to bear the infirmities of the weak, to support them and to be patient and kind toward all men. It's never easy to overlook another's faults or weaknesses, but I believe if we practice doing so we will strengthen our relationships with others.

Chapter 41

Overcome Discouragement, Disillusionment and Deception

Some people pray for things, only to become hurt and angry with God if they don't receive *what* they expected *when* they expected it. These emotions, if allowed to fester, can lead to discouragement, disillusionment and sometimes deception. People who harbor these emotions often focus on feelings of abandonment—believing that God doesn't care about them. Some may even convince themselves that it does no good to pray anymore.

A young woman whose father died of cancer told me, "My dad was a minister who dedicated his whole life to helping people. He prayed for many sick people, and they were healed. Yet, when he was ill and I asked God to heal him and let him live, God let him die. Where was God? Why didn't He heal my dad? God let me down, so I don't believe God is fair or that He loves me. I will not waste my time praying for things, because God will not answer me anyway."

I knew another fellow who was angry and bitter toward God for several years because his brother committed suicide. "I don't understand why God let that happen," he told me. "My dad went to church and was a man of prayer. Why didn't God answer his prayer?"

I hear similar stories frequently, and invariably people conclude that God is unfair because they didn't receive what they expected. Still others believe God doesn't love them anymore. Those people have fallen victim to the original deception; they've listened to Satan's whispers about God. He whispers that God doesn't *really* care, and he suggests that it's useless to talk to God because He's not going to answer.

In John 8:44, the Bible states that Satan is a liar and there is no truth in him: **He was a murderer from the beginning, and abode not in the truth, because there is no truth in him. When he speaketh a lie, he speaketh of his own: for he is a liar, and the father of it.**

Of course, Satan is extremely proficient and practiced at lying, but he doesn't need to say much to discourage Christians who are already negative, who murmur, complain and judge things emotionally. These Christians don't seem to understand that they've focused on their problems more than on God's Word. Therefore, they're emotionally and spiritually vulnerable.

Some may even approach God with a Scripture, stating that they are standing on that particular Scripture for a specific request. I have no doubt the request is as specific as they know how to make it—believing for a job, new car, spouse, health, healing or guidance. And their expectations are specific too. Unfortunately, when they don't see their answers exactly as they want them and when they want them, they act like children, becoming angry with God. They pout and become discouraged and bitter, and they begin to erect walls around themselves, thereby leaving themselves closed to the truth and open to deception.

They haven't truly learned to *know* God or *trust* Him. Psalm 84:11 states, **No good thing will he withhold from them that**

walk uprightly. All of us have unscheduled crises in our lives from time to time. Usually we're not ready for these crises to occur, but if we know and trust God, we can focus on Him and continue to walk uprightly before Him despite the catastrophes. Thus, we establish an atmosphere in which God can perform marvelous miracles in our lives.

Six Reasons Prayers Aren't Answered According to Our Expectations

I believe there are several reasons why prayers are not always answered according to our expectations. I want to discuss six of them, not going into detail but briefly listing them as a guideline or checklist to help when those unscheduled events come. Two reasons prayers aren't always answered have to do with God's sovereign will; two concern our relationship with others; and two have to do with our readiness to receive.

Timing

The first reason our prayers are not always answered according to our expectations is that *it may not be God's timing*. Timing is important to God; He does all things orderly, in season and according to His perfect will. Someone once said, "God is never too early, and He's never too late, but He's always right on time." Many times it seems that He's too late, but He's not. This is not what we want to hear when we're waiting for our answer, but this is where God tests our faith.

It's easy to believe when everything happens according to your timetable. But when things don't come exactly when you expect, and when things go from bad to worse, that's when you know exactly how much you trust God. That's why the apostle

Paul encouraged believers in the Galatian church to keep the faith. He wrote, **And let us not be weary in well doing: for in due season we shall reap, if we faint not** (Gal. 6:9).

The Presence of Strife

The second reason prayers might not be answered when you think they should is *the presence of strife in your life.* The Bible clearly states that if we are embroiled in strife, our prayers *will* be hindered. First Peter 3:7 states, **Likewise, ye husbands, dwell with them according to knowledge, giving honour unto the wife, as unto the weaker vessel, and as being heirs together of the grace of life;** *that your prayers be not hindered.* Or, as *The Living Bible* puts it, **If you don't treat her as you should, your prayers will not get ready answers.**

Obviously, this concept applies to other relationships as well. Peter continues in verses 8 and 9:

> **And now** *this word to all of you:* **You should be like one big happy family, full of sympathy toward each other, loving one another with tender hearts and humble minds. Don't repay evil for evil. Don't snap back at those who say unkind things about you. Instead, pray for God's help for them, for we are to be kind to others, and God will bless us for it.**

Offenses

The third reason our prayers aren't answered when we think they should be is that *an offense has taken root.* A close cousin to strife is offense. Offense is detrimental to our prayer lives, and opportunities for offenses are numerous and inexhaustible. For example, we become offended if perhaps someone borrows something and doesn't return it; if someone fails to shake our hands; if someone misinterprets us; if someone makes a decision we dislike; if someone else gets the position we wanted for ourselves; and the list goes on and on.

While an offense can begin because of something someone else did, it is *you who have the choice to decide how to respond.* Your choices determine whether the windows of heaven are opened for a free flow of blessings upon you or they are locked tightly. God will not unlock those windows of heaven until we become keepers of His Word. And one way to do that is to walk in love with others.

The Bible says in Galatians 5:6 that faith works by love: **For in Jesus Christ neither circumcision availeth any thing, nor uncircumcision; but faith which worketh by love.**

Faith works by love! Walking in love requires that we control our emotions and choose to forgive—always. It's not always easy, but it's as important as any other concept. In fact, this one concept could literally transform your life.

Lack of Spiritual Maturity

The fourth reason our prayers aren't answered when we think they should be is *a lack of spiritual maturity.* When my children were growing up, they would often ask for things I knew they weren't mature enough to handle. When this happened, I acted as a loving parent and decided not to answer their requests lest they hurt themselves.

That's the responsibility of a parent—to judge whether the child is ready to handle something. This judgment should be made in love, not out of anger or meanness.

Likewise, God, our loving Father, knows when we are mature enough to receive our requests. For example, if we cannot yet handle failure, He knows we cannot yet handle success. God can see ahead and determine whether we have any areas of immaturity that we need to deal with. If we aren't ready to receive what we're asking for, God may decide to wait until we grow up before He gives it to us.

Growing up and learning to trust God are a lot like growing up physically. The apostle Paul wrote, "It's like this: When I was a child, I spoke and thought and reasoned as a child does. But when I grew up, I put away childish things." (1 Cor. 13:11.) A good way to test our spiritual maturity levels is to look at how we act when we don't get our way. Do we indulge in pity parties? Do we stay home from church or quit tithing? Do we complain and live carnally just because we've been disappointed? If we become easily disappointed like this, then we aren't spiritually mature and we won't be ready to receive some of the things God has for us.

Wrong Motives

The fifth thing that prevents God from answering prayer is *having wrong motives.* God cares about attitudes and motives. He definitely withholds things that we request if we have wrong motives. The Bible says, **Ye ask, and receive not, because ye ask amiss, that ye may consume it upon your lusts** (James 4:3). Now read that same verse in *The Living Bible:* **And even when you do ask you don't get it because your whole [motive] is wrong—you want only what will give you pleasure.**

One theme in the book of Proverbs is that God weighs our motives. Notice Proverbs 16:2 says that all a man's ways seem innocent to him, but *motives are weighed by the Lord.* Did you know that our motives are those deep and sometimes secret impulses within us that incite action? Therefore, when God weighs our motives, He explores our "life language" just as we study others' "body language" to discover their underlying feelings. Our motives show God how closely attuned we are to His principles.

So, what does God look for when examining our motives? Many things, but I think the primary ones are as follows: (1) We must seek God with our whole hearts; (2) our commitment to God must not be fickle; (3) our requests cannot go against God's Word; and (4) we cannot try to manipulate God.

Isaiah 1:19 says, **If ye be willing and obedient, ye shall eat the good of the land.** Jesus added, **The thing you should want most is God's kingdom and doing what God wants. Then all these other things you need will be given to you** (Matt. 6:33 NCV). Jesus knows that when you seek His kingdom first, you're not going to ask for anything that goes against His Word. As long as your motive is pure, God won't have any problem answering your prayers.

Now let's look at some prayer requests that on the surface look like they should be answered right away, but aren't. Consider, for example, those who come to Christ after living a life of sin, expecting that He will deliver them from the consequences of sin. Make no mistake, Jesus will forgive *sin* unconditionally, but He won't go against His Word. Sometimes the *consequences* of certain sins like adultery and murder must be endured. He will, however, provide the grace to endure those consequences, making them bearable.

Consider those without God who get in trouble financially. But suppose later they come to God and learn to tithe. Often their expectations are that God will get them out of the financial crisis immediately. Sometime He does. However, again, most often He will provide the grace and guidance to walk through the crisis, allowing these people to learn from their mistakes so they can avoid repeating the same problem.

Just remember to maintain a good motive toward God when doing things. When you give out of a pure heart, God will honor it. God's principles work, but only if your motives are pure.

Asking for Things Against God's Will

The sixth thing that prevents God from answering prayer is *when we ask for things that are not His will for us to have.* Often, people ask for things they know God does not want them to have. Nevertheless, they take some Scriptures to stand on and use them to try to make the answer happen. When it doesn't, they may become discouraged.

We should keep in mind that before we ask God for anything, we should know what He thinks about the idea and how it fits into His plan for our lives. If it does not fit with His plan, then He has something else planned. Proverbs 16:1 NCV says, **People may make plans in their minds, but only the Lord can make them come true.**

King David's great dream was to build a temple for the ark of the covenant. He even told the prophet Nathan about his plans, and Nathan gave him the go-ahead, saying, "The Lord is with you." However, Nathan only gave his approval because he loved David and wanted to agree with him. He hadn't really asked God at all. Therefore, based on Nathan's approval, David expected

God to bless him in the building of the temple. God, however, had other plans for David.

That night the Lord said to Nathan, "Go tell David not to build the temple; this is not My plan for him." Hearing that must have been a great disappointment to David, but instead of getting angry and depressed, David remembered all the things God had allowed him to accomplish, and he encouraged himself.

The Bible says,

> **Then King David went in and sat before the Lord, and he said: "Who am I, O Sovereign Lord, and what is my family, that you have brought me this far? And as if this were not enough in your sight, O Sovereign Lord, you have also spoken about the future of the house of your servant. Is this your usual way of dealing with man, O Sovereign Lord? What more can David say to you? For you know your servant, O Sovereign Lord. For the sake of your word and according to your will, you have done this great thing and made it known to your servant. How great you are, O Sovereign Lord! There is no one like you, and there is no God but you, as we have heard with our own ears.**

> **2 Samuel 7:18-22** NIV

David accepted God's will with a great attitude, acknowledging that God knew what he was really like on the inside. If we do the same thing, God will lead us into a better life too. Then we can acknowledge that every day with Jesus is sweeter than the day before.

God always wants the best for us; that's why the Bible says He has plans for us: **For I know the plans I have for you, says** the Lord. They are plans for good and not for evil, to give you a future and a hope. In those days when you pray, I will listen. You will find me when you seek me, if you look for me in earnest (Jer. 29:11-13 TLB).

God's will is for us to have a life full of the following blessings: faith instead of fear; victory instead of depression; confidence instead of doubt; success instead of failure; prosperity instead of poverty; joy and happiness instead of despair.

God is a good God. That may sound simple, but it's true. Therefore, once you realize that He's more than willing to meet your needs, you can rejoice that He'll do it. And if you've been praying for a need that hasn't been answered for one of the six reasons listed above—wrong timing, the presence of strife, offenses, lack of spiritual maturity, wrong motives or asking for things against God's will—don't worry. The next time you pray, just pray in line with God's Word, and you're sure to see your answer.

Chapter 42

Never Leave a Relationship Offended

Some people get offended over the smallest things, and they snoop around, searching for the tiniest mistakes others make—anything at all—to find an excuse to quit a relationship.

Some people leave relationships for odd reasons, saying, for example, "I was bored in the relationship," or, "I had to find myself," or, "He (or she) was dragging me down," or, "I had outgrown that person" or, "He (or she) was not my type, really. I was just being kind to them."

Other people quit jobs for equally odd reasons: "My boss wanted me to work overtime." Or, "My boss never considers that I have a family." That's not the right attitude to take. If you leave a job angry or mad, you'll take that attitude with you wherever you go. You might make excuses, saying, "Well, my boss is a sinner." So what! You're not doing your work unto a person, but unto the Lord. That's the kind of attitude you should take.

In Colossians 3:17,23-25, the apostle Paul explains this principle:

> **And whatsoever ye do in word or deed, do all in the name of the Lord Jesus, giving thanks to God and the Father by him. And whatsoever ye do, do it heartily, as to the Lord, and not unto men; knowing that of the Lord ye shall receive the reward of the inheritance: for**

ye serve the Lord Christ. But he that doeth wrong shall receive for the wrong which he hath done: and there is no respect of persons.

Whatever you think, whatever you say and whatever you do, should be done from the depths of your heart as unto the Lord Jesus. Everything.

This means that when people are snooping around looking for things to criticize or ways to become offended, their attitudes are not pleasing to God. That's wrong. And according to Colossians 3:25, the person who does that will receive discipline.

I can find no justification in the Bible for leaving any relationship offended. It seems to me that God always demands that we straighten out interpersonal conflicts immediately. If we make it a point to never leave any relationship offended, then we will be blessed spiritually, emotionally, physically and socially. It cannot be any other way. The Bible says so. Proverbs 16:7 says, **When a man's ways please the Lord, he** *maketh* **even his enemies to be at peace with him.**

We should leave a relationship, job or church only in God's will. And before leaving, we should ask these questions: *Am I growing here? If not, why? If there's a problem, is it I? Or is it some-one else?* That way, we can determine where a change needs to be made. If it's a problem on our end, then let's admit it, fix it and stay put. We can't let pride cause us to throw away good relationships.

Pride always gets us into trouble when we let it. Notice what the following Scriptures say about pride.

> **Only by pride cometh contention: but with the well advised is wisdom.**
>
> **Proverbs 13:10**

Pride goeth before destruction, and an haughty
spirit before a fall.

Proverbs 16:18

A man's pride shall bring him low: but honour
shall uphold the humble in spirit.

Proverbs 29:23

On the other hand, if you find yourself eager to quit a
relationship or job because of another person's problem, don't
be afraid to confront the person with the right attitude and see if
it can be straightened out. If you find that it cannot be worked
out, then leave without blaming the other person.

It's important to leave a church or relationship in the right
way. You should leave only when you feel God's leading to leave,
not because you can't have your way or because someone or
something has offended you.

When some people quit attending a church they use the
oddest excuses. For example, they may say any of the following:
"Well, I didn't like the way they were treating me." "They would-
n't let me sing." "The pastor's wife didn't speak to me." "The
pastor walked right by me and didn't acknowledge my presence."
"They put that woman in as a teacher? Why didn't they choose
me? I'm better qualified." "Can you imagine? The pastor wanted
him on the board instead of me?"

Not long ago, I noticed a person missing from our congregation. So I called and he told me he couldn't go to church because
he was really busy. I said I understood and accepted his response
to be the truth. However, as time went on and I still didn't see
him, I called again.

"Well, to be honest with you," he said, "I am looking for a different type of ministry. I haven't been getting fed at the church."

In the past, he had said that my style of pastoring had always ministered to him. He'd told me how much he had grown and that the presence of God in our church was awesome. Furthermore, he'd told me that the teaching and ministry led toward growth.

A few days later I asked an associate to call this man and offer help. After he called the man, the story the associate related to me was quite different. He told me that the man had taken some low blows—and they were all aimed at me.

So I called this man back, but he didn't mention what he had told my associate. I tried to draw him out, but he assured me the only reason he had left the church was that he was busy.

I had to take this man at his word, even though I suspected something different. God has really helped me not to take things like that personally and become offended. I just do the best teaching and preaching I can, and I know who I am in Christ. Therefore, I feel like it's his loss, not mine. I told him I didn't take his leaving personally. He had gone from church to church in the past, so I suspected he would never find the perfect church.

Another time this happened, and it involved a man who worked directly with me. All at once, he began to drop out of the work scene. And when I asked him where he'd been, he always gave me excuses. However, I realized he had gotten offended and was hiding behind those excuses.

One day at lunch during some small talk, I asked him if he was offended by anything.

"No, not at all," he said. "Everything is just fine."

"Well, where have you been?"

"Well, I'm busy doing this and that."

Somehow, I knew he was not being completely truthful, but I walked away trying to accept what he had told me as truth. I still hoped we could maintain a good relationship.

A couple of weeks later, he told several of his good friends that he was indeed offended. But pride on his part kept us apart. He deprived himself of being around people he loved and who loved him. More than that, however, he covered it up and blamed someone else for an offense he was harboring.

By harboring an offense against me, this man was keeping God's blessings from himself. The Bible says, **Know ye not, that to whom ye yield yourselves servants to obey, his servants ye are to whom ye obey; whether of sin unto death, or of obedience unto righteousness?** (Rom. 6:16).

So both of these men became offended and left the church. But instead of telling the truth, they gave excuses for leaving. They allowed themselves to get offended over some small things instead of dealing with the problems. They blamed their reactions on God, saying, "He is leading me somewhere else," when, in fact, this was not the truth. Nevertheless, they refused to deal with the offense and went on to other churches.

If someone has done you a wrong turn, causing you to think about leaving a church, think again. If you leave that way, you will face the same kind of problem elsewhere. *The way you leave a church or relationship is the way you will enter the next one.* If you're offended when you leave the first church or relationship, you will probably have a worse time in the new church or relationship. Moreover, if you're running from your problems, harboring unforgiveness toward someone, God will not forgive you.

Don't let pride and unforgiveness keep you from the many blessings God has for you. Jesus said, **When ye stand praying, forgive, if ye have aught against any: that your Father also which is in heaven may forgive you your trespasses. But if ye do not forgive, neither will your Father which is in heaven forgive your trespasses** (Mark 11:25,26).

I am amazed at the reasons people usually give for leaving churches. Most of them boil down to the truth that they did not get their own way. Then they get hurt and offended, so they begin making up reasons to get out.

One of the most popular excuses I hear people giving for leaving a church is that they aren't growing. The truth is that many times they aren't growing because they're harboring offenses. That's why most church-hopping occurs. If people aren't truthful about their reasons for leaving, they've already built walls of offenses.

When this happens, I've learned it's best to let go. If I happen to see someone who is offended, I won't ignore that person or become rude. What good would that do? That person has already made his or her choice. Besides, God is my source, so why should I be bothered if someone leaves and isn't honest about the reason? That is that person's problem, not mine.

I know some pastors who really have a hard time with people who leave like this. Some pastors are rude about it too. They often won't speak to people who leave their churches. That's wrong, and it's certainly not setting a good example.

Some pastors are too proud to accept any kind of correction whatsoever. That's wrong, but we must be careful not to judge one minister by the mistakes of another. When someone leaves a church, the new pastor will need time to get to know that person. Also, that new person will have to get used to another church all over again.

Usually, the way someone leaves a church relationship is the same way they leave personal relationships. The thing to remember is that this practice is wrong. Therefore, instead of letting offenses take root and drive us from an otherwise good church or personal relationship, let's take time to deal with the offense. Making things right is always the best thing to do.

Chapter 43

Grieving Inordinately Is Holding Onto Something You No Longer Have

Despite our best efforts, relationships sometimes fall apart. When this happens, we often grieve if we try to hang on to them. It's tormenting to a person with whom another tries to salvage a relationship. This is a bad practice and should be avoided. Nevertheless, it is natural to grieve when something is lost. Yet it's wrong to grieve beyond a certain point.

Nehemiah told the children of Israel to quit grieving because the joy of the Lord was their strength. (Neh. 8:10.) Well, if the joy of the Lord was *their* strength, then it's *our* strength too. No matter what happens, the joy of the Lord is our strength. We may have lost a friend, a job or a loved one, but we need not grieve inordinately or become extremely depressed. Instead, we can practice a joyful attitude with God. We can start by saying yes to the good things from Christ Jesus on the inside of us. We can stop vacillating between up and down, in and out, and backwards and forwards. And we can start rising up in the power of the Holy Ghost, allowing Jesus Christ to be our Lord, our stronghold and our strength.

Well, how do we go about practicing these things? In a broken relationship, it starts by forgiving the person who left. It's not necessary for us to understand why that person left or even what caused the relationship to break up. It's only necessary to forgive and ask forgiveness. This is not always easy, but if we ask God, He will enable us to release any emotional attachment.

Once we've forgiven the person who hurt us, the next step is to prevent bitterness from taking root in our hearts. This may be a full-time job that requires vigilance, persistence and a lot of prayer.

Finally, to prevent inordinate grieving, we must move forward, leaving our depression behind. By admitting we can't hold on to something, we free ourselves to move forward and get on with life.

PART VIII

Avoid
Relationships
That Kill

Chapter 44

Selfishness

The French call one disease *La Maladie du moi*, or "me-sickness." Many of us are troubled with this disease; we are too concerned with ourselves. Despite all the advances we've made in science and in social reform, no one has discovered a vaccine for this ailment.

Selfishness, or me-sickness, can be a big hindrance in any relationship. Selfishness is that stubborn quality that insists on having its own way. It is the need to be right, to get what we want out of a relationship, rather than giving to it. The apostle Paul condemns selfishness in 1 Corinthians 10:24 AMP: **Let not one then seek his own good and advantage and profit, but [rather let him seek the welfare of his neighbor] each one of the other.**

I saw an example of this kind of giving during a ministers' convention not too long ago. I was so moved by what I saw that I sat and wept. The convention host got up to speak, and he was carrying a big sack with him. He reached in and started pulling items from the sack right in front of everybody. He took out books and tape sets from the various speakers in attendance at the convention. He promised to give everyone who registered for the convention a copy of each book and tape set. He continued to empty the entire sack, which was filled with other ministers' material. When he had finished, I realized there was nothing from his ministry on the stage. The sack was filled entirely with the literature of others.

I wept because of this minister's humility and the manner in which he selflessly conducted himself. He was probably the best-known of the ministers, but he treated all the others as equals, giving them credibility through his introduction. He wasn't seeking his own glory, advantage or profit. He did not imply, "I'm the great man of God here, and all of these others are just subordinates."

By giving the literature of others to the people at his own convention, and by allowing the other ministers to be promoted instead of himself, he was saying, "I look up to these men."

This attitude is admirable and should be evidenced in every area of our lives. The nature of godliness runs contrary to selfishness. Someone once said, "Thinking only of oneself is really a living hell." The great Sam Jones said, "Hell is selfishness on fire."

In the Garden of Gethsemane, Jesus prayed, "Not My will but Yours be done." (Matt 26:39.) From a selfish standpoint, it would have been better for Jesus personally to avoid the ordeal of the Cross. But Jesus wasn't thinking of Himself. He knew a price had to be paid for man's redemption and restoration into fellowship with God, and He was willing to pay it.

Fortunately, you and I don't have to go to the cross as Jesus did. We do, however, have to crucify the flesh. We must put self in its place, making Jesus the Lord of our lives. It is only when we abandon ourselves to the love God engenders that we can cure me-sickness.

Chapter 45

Self-Pity

In the Charles Dickens book, *David Copperfield*, Mrs. Gummidge laments, "I am a lone lorn creetur and everythink goes contrairy with me."[1]

I heard of a pastor once who got into this same habit of murmuring and complaining in an attitude of self-pity. Whenever anything happened that did not go his way, he'd shout, "Oh great!" in a persecuted sort of way. Soon, God began to convict him of his bad attitude, and every time he shouted, "Oh great!" the Holy Spirit would whisper, *What about Romans 8:28?*

Now, the pastor tried to ignore the still, small voice of the Holy Spirit, but he could not. One day during prayer, he flipped open his Bible and read Romans 8:28: **And we know that all things work together for good to them that love God, to them who are the called according to his purpose.**

The Holy Spirit continued to talk to him this way. *I said, "All things work together for good,"* whispered the Holy Spirit, *but, whenever something happens that you don't like, you yell, "Oh great!"*

When he heard that, the pastor was gripped by his display of self-pity and determined to change. For the next several months, whenever this man started to yell, "Oh great!" he would deliberately add the words, "is thy faithfulness." And eventually he turned his murmuring self-pity into a shout of praise! He changed a lament into a praise.

It's true, however, that none of us is immune to self-pity from time to time. It usually shows up as an excuse to fret about some alleged wrong done to us. David wrote, **Stop your anger! Turn off your wrath. Don't fret and worry—it only leads to harm** (Ps. 37:8 TLB).

Asaph, one of David's court musicians and the author of Psalm 73, experienced the destructive forces of fretting. He wrote, **But as for me, my feet had almost slipped: I had nearly lost my foothold. For I envied the arrogant when I saw the prosperity of the wicked** (vv. 2,3 NIV). Asaph explained how he went on to brood over his envy of the prosperity of the wicked. Finally, he brought himself into deep despair and rebellion against God. Notice verse 16, **When I tried to understand all this, it was oppressive to me.**

Caught in a vortex of self-pity, Asaph became embittered, suffering great anguish. He wrote, **When my heart was grieved and my spirit embittered, I was senseless and ignorant; I was a brute beast before you** (vv. 21,22). Not until he repented and reached out to God did he find relief (v. 17) and counsel (vv. 24-26).

Indulging in self-pity is not a solitary action. Those who practice it play off the responses of others. Outbursts of self-pity frequently turn into gripe sessions and full-fledged pity parties. Griping, in turn, feeds misery; and misery soon leads to slanderous attacks on others. Obviously these attacks can be devastating to relationships.

Self-pity can also be highly self-destructive. In fact, it is generally the first step in a downward spiral of self-destruction. If not checked, that downward spiral can move from self-pity to anger, to bitterness, to depression and finally suicide. Therefore, it is important to identify the cycle and break it as quickly as possible.

One of the best ways to break the destructive spiral of self-pity is to substitute biblical alternatives for negative thoughts. One biblical thought that comes to mind is found in Psalm 37. David instructs us not to fret over or envy evildoers. Instead, we can supplant those insecure thoughts with the following biblical thoughts: (1) trusting in the Lord, (2) delighting ourselves in the Lord, (3) committing our ways to the Lord, (4) becoming still, (5) waiting patiently for Him and (6) refraining from anger. These are six alternatives to fretting and envying.

In order to substitute bad thoughts with biblical thoughts, it is necessary to search the Scriptures. It would be a good idea to mark these Scriptures in your Bible so you are constantly reminded of them. The more often you substitute biblical thoughts for negative thoughts or actions that are displeasing to God, the more you will please Him. Eventually, you can reach the place where you automatically substitute the biblical thought for the negative thought.

It's so sad that many Christians carry around problems and bad attitudes when they don't have to. They're like the elder brother of the prodigal son, thinking they do everything right. (Luke 15:11-32.) The elder brother chose to stay home. There was no way he was going to leave home and sow wild oats. And, when the younger brother came home, the elder brother's bad attitude began to surface. First, he felt self-important. Then, he got mad and started complaining.

The prodigal son's brother indulged in feelings of self-pity. He said to his father, "All these years I've been faithful. I've never neglected you; I've always done what you told me, but you've never given me a party so I could have a good time with my friends."

The elder brother's attitude reveals three negative thought patterns, which are listed below:

1. **The prodigal's brother assumed the place and privilege of a son but neglected the responsibility of a brother.** Outwardly he was correct, conscientious, industrious and dutiful, but inwardly he was selfish and resentful. These feelings resulted in a bad relationship with his younger brother and a strained relationship with his father.

2. **The prodigal's brother didn't serve his father with his whole heart.** Had he served with the right heart attitude, he would have maintained fellowship with his father, cultivating similar interests with him. Yet it seems the elder brother didn't really know his father. He really had no idea why his father rejoiced so much over his younger son's return.

3. **The prodigal's brother couldn't enjoy the things he did have.** It is possible to be heir to everything your father possesses and still be unhappy. Even the servants were happier than the older son was. They ate, laughed and danced while he stood outside demanding his rights. A bad attitude kept the elder brother away from the good things his father wanted to bless him with.

Harboring bad attitudes will block the blessings of God and prevent you from apprehending God's plan and realizing your full potential.

In the parable of the prodigal son, I see two prodigals, not one. The younger brother was guilty of sins of the flesh, but the elder brother was guilty of sins of the spirit. At the end of the parable, it is the elder brother—the second prodigal—who is outside the father's house.

If we ever develop a bad attitude like the prodigal's elder brother, we should remember the following things:

1. Our privilege.

    Son, thou art ever with me (Luke 15:31).

2. Our possessions.

    All that I have is thine (Luke 15:31).

You see, if we live our lives looking out only for ourselves and our own personal interests, we become like the elder brother. Nurturing attitudes of self-importance, self-pity, jealousy and selfishness will only harm us and cause us to miss the blessings God has for us.

Chapter 46

Fear of Rejection

At some point in their lives, all believers have to deal with the fear of rejection. Being born again and experiencing the new life of Jesus Christ is great, but it doesn't automatically keep the old nature from creeping up sometimes.

Even Jesus faced the heart-wrenching feeling of rejection. The Bible says,

> He was despised and rejected and forsaken by men, a Man of sorrows and pains, and acquainted with grief and sickness; and as one from Whom men hide their faces He was despised, and we did not appreciate His worth or have any esteem for Him.
>
> Surely He has borne our griefs, sickness, weakness and distress—and carried our sorrows and pain [of punishment]. Yet we ignorantly considered Him stricken, smitten and afflicted by God [as if with leprosy].
>
> But He was wounded for our transgressions, He was bruised for our guilt and iniquities; the chastisement needful to obtain peace and well-being for us was upon Him, and with the stripes that wounded Him we are healed and made whole.
>
> **Isaiah 53:3-5** AMP

Take a moment and reread these verses and look for words that describe rejection: "despised," "forsaken," "sorrows," "pains," "men hid their faces from Him," "[they] did not appreciate His worth."

Yes, I believe Jesus understands what it feels like to suffer rejection.

The fear of rejection is an outgrowth of one of our greatest legitimate needs—the need to be accepted. The good news is that Jesus accepts us when we accept Him. He even accepts us with our hang-ups and shortcomings. He knows that we're all different—not weird or wrong, just different. Nevertheless, He still loves us, because He sees us as cleansed by His blood.

If only we could be so forgiving with our friends. Even though we love our friends, they sometimes may not be able to receive it. Consequently, we may feel rejected. Furthermore, we may develop a fear of rejection, which is sometimes difficult for us to overcome.

I want to list a few things that can cause a fear of rejection, and I will give brief explanations of why they do.

Insecure parents. By some mysterious process, parents who are insecure seem to pass along their fear of rejection to their children, and sometimes this continues for several generations.

Arguments between parents. Even though arguments between parents may occur behind closed doors, children usually know it's happening. When parents argue harshly, fear of rejection can creep into a child's heart.

Abusive parents. Parents who call their children names, verbally put them down, make unreasonable demands, yell and scream or punish harshly are abusing their children. Children can be abused physically, emotionally, mentally and spiritually.

God says your children are a heritage from the Lord, which indicates that you should cherish them, not abuse them.

Abuse by others. Loving parents never allow anyone to abuse their children. Parents need to stick up for their children and protect them from harmful people.

Dysfunctional homes. It is vitally important that parents show love and acceptance for each member of their family. It's also important that parents learn to cooperate and to live together in peace.

Divorce and broken homes. When families part ways, it's difficult to prevent feelings of rejection. These feelings can overwhelm all those involved. Sometimes families find it difficult to differentiate between the problems and the people. Children, in particular, often feel as though they caused the divorce and that their parents are casting them away. Therefore, it is of paramount importance that divorced parents give their children lots of love and reassurance of their acceptance.

Unfaithfulness in marriage. Most people go into marriage expecting "to live happily ever after." When this doesn't happen, some people look elsewhere for happiness. Discovering that a spouse has been unfaithful is devastating. It can flood everyone involved with feelings of inadequacy, imperfection and unworthiness. Infidelity can cause untold pain and must be avoided at all costs.

These are only some of the causes of rejection. But it's enough to give you an idea of how your actions affect the lives of those around you.

Now let's look at the results of the fear of rejection and what emotions it can lead into.

Self-pity. This first step in the downward cycle of self-destruction must be broken immediately. As we discussed in the previous chapter, we cannot afford to indulge in feelings of self-pity.

Poor self-image. This is a negative emotion caused by the embroiled feelings of rejection. Remember who you are in Christ and look at yourself as being worthy.

Loneliness. Feelings of rejection often cause loneliness. Don't let loneliness prevent you from reaching out to others in friendship.

Fear. The feeling of rejection can lead to feelings of fear. Don't allow fear to paralyze your life.

Guilt. This is a feeling that can result from social suggestions, a fear of taboos or losing the love of others.

Bitterness. Bitterness can result from *any* unforgiven offense that has taken root in the heart and produces a crop of unresolved feelings such as anger, bitterness and hurt.

Hopelessness. The fear of rejection can lead to such despair and dejection that one who experiences it feels a real sense of hopelessness.

Disrespect. Often when one feels that he will be rejected, he covers his fear by treating another person with disrespect. It's as though he feels that treating someone with respect makes him vulnerable to rejection.

Rebellion. This is just one step beyond disrespect in the degenerative process. When someone feels he will be rejected, he may deliberately choose to rebel against authority.

Jealousy. Jealousy affects both men and women, particularly those who are insecure. When one feels he cannot safely trust those he loves, he may respond with jealousy.

233

Competition. Feelings of self-worth and security should come from God, not from an occupation. A competitive attitude can isolate one from others.

I remember when I first entered the ministry. It seemed that all the preachers around me were comparing the sizes of their tents and the frequencies of their broadcasts. They seemed to feel that this was more important than the message they preached. This attitude is sometimes caused by a fear of rejection.

Anorexia and other eating disorders. Eating disorders can range from anorexia to gluttony. The size of the person is not an indicator of whether he or she has an eating disorder. I've seen skinny gluttons, and I'm sure you have too.

Most of us find comfort in eating. Therefore, when we fear something, it's somewhat normal for us to turn to eating. The extremes are what hurt us; therefore, we should seek a balance in our eating.

Membership in gangs. Not too long ago, I read in the newspaper about a teenaged gang member who committed murder. We have this problem in many cities. Too often, young people feel rejected by family or peers, so they join gangs to find acceptance and self-esteem. Unfortunately, little good ever comes from these associations.

These are just a few of the outgrowths of rejection. I'm sure there are others, but these are enough to give you an idea of how far-reaching its effects are. Now I want to show you how to get rid of the fear of rejection.

Cures for the Fear of Rejection

First of all, deal with yourself through the Holy Spirit. Recognize that you are the righteousness of God in Christ. That means you can become cleansed by Jesus' blood and by walking in fellowship with Him.

First John 4:18 says, **There is no fear in love; but perfect love casteth out fear: because fear hath torment. He that feareth is not made perfect in love.** Fear brings thoughts of punishment, but when we realize Jesus has already taken our punishment, we are no longer subject to fear. This revelation of how much God loves us is the number-one cure for feelings of rejection.

Even though it may not always feel like it, God accepts you. It's all right to be different.

Here are some basic principles to follow for overcoming the fear of rejection:

1. Your foundation determines the quality of your life. If the Word of God is your foundation, your life will exemplify goodness, trust, love and integrity. If the values of the world are your foundation, you may expect anything on a constantly shifting basis.

2. The way people treat you does not determine your value. Your value is found in Jesus Christ alone.

3. Your security is not in your job, money, education, social standing, marital status or children. Only in Jesus Christ is there everlasting security.

In Romans 8:35-39 AMP, Paul describes our source of security:

> **Who shall ever separate us from Christ's love? Shall suffering and affliction and tribulation? Or calamity and distress? Or persecution, or hunger, or destitution, or peril, or sword?**

Even as it is written, "For Thy sake we are put to death all the day long, we are regarded and counted as sheep for the slaughter."

Yet amid all these things we are more than conquerors and gain a surpassing victory through Him Who loved us.

For I am persuaded beyond doubt—am sure—that neither death, nor life, nor angels, nor principalities, nor things impending and threatening, nor things to come, nor powers, nor height, nor depth, nor anything else in all creation will be able to separate us from the love of God which is in Christ Jesus our Lord.

Meditate on these Scriptures and let these words comfort you. Overcoming the fear of rejection is possible, and it can be done with perseverance and help from God and His Word.

Chapter 47

Pride, Arrogance and an Overbearing Manner

Pride is a destructive force. Proverbs 16:18-19 AMP says, **Pride goes before destruction, and a haughty spirit before a fall. Better it is to be a humble spirit with the meek and poor, than to divide the spoil with the proud.**

It's amazing how people allow themselves to be caught up in pride. There were times when pride was a part of my life. And it took me a while, but I finally realized that pride can be a spirit of the devil that tries to make me fall. But I don't have to succumb to the spirit of pride.

I've learned to be who I am. For example, when I'm talking with people at a convention or meeting, I don't try to impress them by telling them how many times I've preached in big meetings. That doesn't help me.

We need to be who we are; we need to walk in humility. By walking in humility, we display Christ's character within us. Conversely, when we walk in pride, we're not being ourselves; our walk is false. And sooner or later, our true nature will surface and we'll be found out.

I have a friend who has lots of money, but I don't go around telling people that he's my friend. He doesn't give me any of his money; his money doesn't help me at all. I'm not in that relationship for the money. I'm not going around telling people I'm this man's friend because he has money. That's pride, and it's wrong.

I've seen people who are always trying to build themselves up by letting others know who their friends are, but it really isn't necessary.

That's not walking in humility; that's walking in pride. And pride is the first of the seven things that God hates.

Let's go over the list in Proverbs 6:16-19 of the seven things God hates:

> These six things doth the Lord hate: yea, seven are an abomination unto him: A proud look, a lying tongue, and hands that shed innocent blood, an heart that deviseth wicked imaginations, feet that be swift in running to mischief, a false witness that speaketh lies, and he that soweth discord among brethren.

Throughout the book of Proverbs, we are shown pride's adverse effects on a person's life and on his or her relationships. Let's look at several examples in the book of Proverbs.

> When pride comes, then comes disgrace, but with humility comes wisdom.
>
> Proverbs 11:2 NIV

> Better to be a nobody and yet have a servant than pretend to be somebody and have no food.
>
> Proverbs 12:9 NIV

One man pretends to be rich, yet has nothing; another pretends to be poor, yet has great wealth.

Proverbs 13:7 NIV

Pride only breeds quarrels, but wisdom is found in those who take advice.

Proverbs 13:10 NIV

The Lord tears down the proud man's house but he keeps the widow's boundaries intact.

Proverbs 15:25 NIV

The Lord detests all the proud of heart. Be sure of this: They will not go unpunished.

Proverbs 16:5 NIV

Pride goes before destruction, a haughty spirit before a fall. Better to be lowly in spirit and among the oppressed than to share plunder with the proud.

Proverbs 16:18,19 NIV

Before his downfall a man's heart is proud, but humility comes before honor.

Proverbs 18:12 NIV

It is not fitting for a fool to live in luxury—how much worse for a slave to rule over princes!

Proverbs 19:10 NIV

Who can say, "I have kept my heart pure; I am clean and without sin"?

Proverbs 20:9 NIV

Haughty eyes and a proud heart, the lamp of the wicked, are sin!

Proverbs 21:4 NIV

The proud and arrogant man—"Mocker" is his name; he behaves with overweening pride.

Proverbs 21:24 NIV

Humility and the fear of the Lord bring wealth and honor and life.

Proverbs 22:4 NIV

It is not good to eat too much honey, nor is it honorable to seek one's own honor.

Proverbs 25:27 NIV

The sluggard is wiser in his own eyes than seven men who answer discreetly.

Proverbs 26:16 NIV

Let another praise you, and not your own mouth; someone else, and not your own lips.

Proverbs 27:2 NIV

The crucible for silver and the furnace for gold, but man is tested by the praise he receives.

Proverbs 27:21 NIV

A man's pride brings him low, but a man of lowly spirit gains honor.

Proverbs 29:23 NIV

In addition to these many references to pride in the book of Proverbs, notice what the apostle Paul says about pride in Romans 12:3-10 NIV:

> For by the grace given me I say to every one of you: *Do not think of yourself more highly than you ought, but rather think of yourself with sober judgment, in accordance with the measure of faith God has given you.*
>
> Just as each of us has one body with many members, and these members do not all have the same function, so in Christ we who are many form one body, and each member belongs to all the others.
>
> We have different gifts, according to the grace given us. If a man's gift is prophesying, let him use it in proportion to his faith. If it is serving, let him serve; if it is teaching, let him teach; if it is encouraging, let him encourage; if it is contributing to the needs of others, let him give generously; if it is leadership, let him govern diligently; if it is showing mercy, let him do it cheerfully. Love must be sincere.
>
> Hate what is evil; cling to what is good. *Be devoted to one another in brotherly love. Honor one another above yourselves.*

Much could be said about the human tendency to exaggerate one's own worth or importance in an overbearing manner, but I'm confident that the above Scriptures already demonstrate how this tendency can damage relationships.

Perhaps because it's difficult for most people to prefer one another and to love one another, Jesus Christ chose that test to determine true discipleship. He said, **By this shall all men** know that ye are my disciples, if ye have love one to another (John 13:35).

PART IX

Strengthen Your
Relationship
With God and
the Church

Chapter 48

Yield to
the Spirit
of God

We cannot be effective for God or in touching the lives of others until we acknowledge the good things within us that come from Jesus Christ. In the short letter Paul wrote to Philemon about the runaway slave, Onesimus, he instructs Philemon and us to share our faith with others. Philemon 6 TLB says, **And I pray that as you share your faith with others it will grip their lives too, as they see the wealth of good things in you that come from Christ Jesus.**

These good things which come from Christ Jesus enable us to withstand the trials and persecutions that come our way. They enable us to choose to be good friends, and they enable us to walk in a way that is pleasing to God. However, when somebody spews forth bad things about us, our old flesh wants to stand up and say, "I'm not guilty. I didn't do that." Usually, we want to rise up and take revenge.

But that's the time to rise up, crucify the flesh and say, **Blessed are they which are persecuted for righteousness' sake: for theirs is the kingdom of heaven** (Matt. 5:10).

If we are going to have good relationships, be prosperous and enjoy life, we must daily bring the flesh under subjection. We must also understand and obey the laws of God.

After we do this, we can read them the law, go our way, as Nehemiah told the children of Israel and, **Eat the fat, and drink the sweet, and send portions unto them for whom nothing is prepared: for this day is holy unto our Lord: neither be ye sorry; for the joy of the Lord is your strength** (Neh. 8:10). We can rise up every morning, asking, "To whom can I reach out or speak God's encouragement? Whom can I bless?"

Unfortunately, too many of us wake up and say, "I hope somebody gives me a word today." However, if we want someone to give us a word, we should start giving out kind words to others first and start acting like Jesus.

All of this begins with yielding to the Spirit of God. It also involves laying everything on God's altar, beginning with us. God doesn't want our money or our service first; He wants us. Look at 2 Corinthians 8:5: **And this** [the Macedonian Christians] **did, not as we hoped, but first gave their own selves to the Lord, and unto us by the will of God.**

Having placed ourselves on the altar, we should then bring our loved ones to Him, surrendering our rights to them. For example, should God wish to use our children in foreign missions, we should whisper, "Thy will be done, Lord." Should God call us to work in another state, away from our children or friends, we should again whisper, "Thy will be done, Lord."

Once we've yielded to the Spirit of God, we should never again desire to use our talents, time or money for any worldly purpose.

Making money, impressing people and gaining power should become less important to us. Instead, we should seek the Lord's blessings and approval. Finally, our plans, ambitions, dreams and aspirations must be laid on God's altar. His will should become ours. His plan for our lives should become our plan.

Our future and all of our relationships are in His hands. When everything is in His hands, we are truly yielded to the Spirit of God and have no reason to be grieved or depressed.

Chapter 49

Deal With Unresolved Issues

A common unrealistic expectation held by many new Christians is that all of their problems and unresolved issues will disappear as soon as they are born again. They commonly think all of their hurts and wounds of the past will be instantly healed and that life will forever be perfect and rosy. This expectation underscores a lack of understanding about the new birth and its effects on one's life.

The new birth is a new beginning, a starting place. But it's the beginning of a process called sanctification. Like any birth, the one being born begins a process, at that very moment, of learning to be and to act like the rest of his species. He also begins a process of overcoming difficulties and obstacles peculiar to his species.

For example, the human baby begins the process of learning to sit, to crawl, to stand, to walk and then to run. He must learn to feed himself, to communicate with others and to care for himself. Sometimes, as when there are birth defects, the human child must overcome incredible obstacles, often at unbelievable odds, to do ordinary activities. Even for those without such great challenges, it is not deemed unusual that the process of maturing consumes years. We simply label those years as infancy, childhood, middle years and teenage years. We expect progress, failure, restarts and finally success.

Sadly though, when this process is applied to a spiritual new birth, we expect instant perfection. This does not automatically happen. Each of us must continue to deal with issues. Most often, as in the process of ordinary human growth, we learn to face these challenges and overcome them.

In the maturing years overcoming obstacles becomes the focus of the Christian walk, which is less a religion than a way of life. It is a way of facing and overcoming obstacles that hamper spiritual growth. The surest way of ensuring spiritual growth is to apply the principles in God's Word to each element of daily life. This application is easier to accomplish when one understands his three-part being: body, soul and spirit.

The new birth occurs in our spirits when God resides within us. He begins to guide us in the renewing of our minds in accordance with His Word. The soul, with its memories of the past and former soul ties, must be broken. The soul will often resist and cling to destructive and subversive behaviors, generally expressed through feelings of guilt, unworthiness and denial. Dealing with bodily applications is more straightforward. Each of us has developed physical habits and addictions that are counterproductive to spiritual growth. These behaviors, in turn, must be replaced with godly principles and actions. It is often hard work to replace bad habits with desirable ones, but through regular persistence, this can be done.

A good example of someone who exchanged his bad habits for good ones is found in an account presented by a man in one of our Canadian crusades, who related how he had been involved in pornography for much of his adult life. After he became a Christian, he was troubled with pornographic images flooding his mind, particularly when he wished to praise God. Feeling ashamed and guilty, he did all he knew to do to get rid of the images. He asked God to take the pictures out of his mind; he rebuked the devil; he prayed for deliverance. Nothing seemed to work. For five years, he was afraid to tell anyone what he was experiencing. His mental anguish was particularly poignant when he listened to ministers preach from 2 Corinthians 5:17 NKJV: **Therefore, if anyone is in Christ, he is a new creation; old things have passed away; behold, all things have become new.**

Old things had not passed away in his life; all things were not new. Doubts about whether his conversion was genuine plagued him. Yet he knew that he had confessed his sin and was no longer involved in pornography. Although he loved God with all of his heart, he was tormented by these mental images every time he went to church. After five years in the church, he had to turn down requests to serve in various positions because of his problem, although no one knew his reasons for declining proffered positions in the church. He simply couldn't seem to get any help.

As many ministers had instructed from the pulpit, he read and meditated on the Word of God, even memorizing and quoting several Scriptures on a regular basis, particularly Romans 12:1-2 NKJV:

> **I beseech you therefore, brethren, by the mercies of God, that you present your bodies a living sacrifice, holy, acceptable to God, which is your reasonable service. And do not be conformed to this world, but be transformed by the renewing of your mind, that you**

**may prove what is that good and acceptable and
perfect will of God.**

He was doing all he knew to do to promote spiritual healing
and growth, but nothing seemed to work.

Sometimes hurts and wounds of the past are so deeply embed-
ded in our hearts that a healing first requires a desire for healing,
then the Holy Spirit's guidance, time spent in the Word and prayer
and finally a spiritual mentor who will disciple and guide us.

Those are the steps this man finally took. Once he asked for
help, we were able to work with him to set him free from those
tormenting images. Today, he is no longer ashamed, because
God has taken these images from him.

Many people live with all kinds of leftover issues stuffed away
inside that they are trying to hide. Oftentimes, however, instead
of dealing with these issues themselves, they expect God to
automatically erase all of their pain. They forget they themselves
are the ones in charge of their own spiritual growth.

Just as the human baby undergoes normal stages of development on his own, so must we continue to develop the spirit man
within. Otherwise, eventually these issues will erupt and cause
problems in the future.

For example, one woman I know confessed that her father
had sexually abused her for a number of years. And although she
told her mother what her father was doing, her mother refused
to believe her. Finally, when she was old enough, she left home
with a deep hatred for both of her parents.

Years later, when this woman became a Christian, she
expected the hatred to instantly disappear, but it didn't. Deeply
tormented by her persistent hatred, she was afraid to share her
feelings with anyone for years, always mindful of the remarkable

testimonies from others who had been freed from similar circumstances. She knew she loved God and had let go of her past, but somehow her hatred toward her parents tormented her day and night.

Finally, after a lot of soul searching, she went to her parents and expressed her forgiveness. Afterwards, for the first time, she felt peace. During a meeting where I happened to be ministering she testified to the immediate change.

At the same meeting, another young man shared how he had been molested as a young boy. The experience had damaged him emotionally, and he was too ashamed to tell anyone because he was afraid no one would believe him. Consequently, he just kept it to himself. He later married and had two children, and although he had always been faithful to his wife, the devil tormented him with thoughts that he was gay. The guilt and torturous thoughts that ensued were so severe that he often thought he could not continue serving God.

He thought he wasn't like other Christians, who seemed to always be free and enjoy the blessings of God. He felt like giving up so many times. He knew the old things had not passed away from his life, nor was everything new. It was only after hearing the testimonies of others Christians who had experienced similar things and had believed God for deliverance and guidance and learned how to follow Him that he understood this was the only way to rid himself of the connection to his past.

Everywhere I go, Christians tell me about the anger they carry inside. They talk about how they had expected it to be erased at the new birth, but how it has plagued them even afterward. I've been able to explain how the anger is forgiven, and they've worked through it with the help of God's Word and by admitting to others that they need help.

The wife in one married couple I counseled told me she was afraid of her husband's violent temper and his resulting rages. Generally, she said, he was a good, kind man who prayed with her and attended church. They were regular tithers and volunteered to help on many projects. But rage would always overtake him.

During our conversation, I began to question the husband about his past. I learned something terrible. As a boy he had actually killed his father in order to protect his mother from his father's abuse. Needless to say, this was a major issue for him to overcome.

As we talked, he realized he needed to take control of his life and allow the Holy Spirit help him heal. This was difficult for him because he had never told anyone about these things from his past. He had been too ashamed to ask for help, yet he didn't know how to deal with them himself.

It took this man some time, patience, self-control and godly intervention, but he finally received his deliverance and is a free man today.

I often ask people who have uncontrollable anger to come forward in my meetings for prayer. I'm always surprised to see how many respond. This tells me these people have never let Jesus become Lord of their lives in that area. If they had, these issues would not still be present. You see, when people allow Jesus to become Lord in the problem areas, He can help them heal.

When anger resides inside a person who was regularly mistreated in the past, and someone mistreats him now, the anger which has built up over the years causes the person to react to an entire history of injustice rather than to just the present incident. But God can help move the person through the problem to a spiritually mature state in which the pain is healed and the person grows to be more and more like Jesus Christ.

People in Leadership

The church should be viewed as a place in which God's mercy and grace reside, not as a place that is free of problems. All churches face problems from time to time. For example, just because someone holds a leadership position in a church does not guarantee that the person is spiritually mature or is even necessarily qualified to hold that position.

We usually expect a spiritual leader to demonstrate a positive attitude, a godly character, a thorough knowledge of biblical principles and experience in overcoming tests and temptations. Sadly, however, this is not always the case. On the other hand, it does not mean that all leaders in a given church are underqualified either.

Church leaders are human too. Some have never dealt with their own unresolved issues. Others hide their problems and lead double lives until eventually their sins become revealed. Furthermore, it's possible some may feel they cannot confess their problems to anyone because they think no one would understand or keep a confidence. That is usually Satan's way of keeping people in bondage. Eventually, however, secrets have a way of surfacing and the person may find he must deal with the issue publicly anyway. Therefore, it's important to choose confidences carefully. But, more importantly, it's best to deal with unresolved issues early.

A young man once came to my office because his wife had handed him an ultimatum—either he had to talk to me about some issues that were dividing them, or she would leave him. Therefore, because he didn't want to lose his marriage, he came and talked with me.

At first we only beat around the bush, chatting about trivial things. After spending too much time on side issues, I finally told him that if he refused to share his problems with me, then I could not help him. It was then that he told me his parents had taught him to keep all personal matters private, which made it very difficult for him to talk about such things.

I told him I understood what he had been taught and that he should not go around indiscriminately telling people about his personal problems. But I also told him he could trust me, and I assured him that what he told me would be kept in confidence. I also said that I couldn't help him until we talked.

Soon he felt relieved enough to begin telling me his problems, which included things he had carried inside him ever since becoming a Christian. As a result of our conversation, he was able to receive a breakthrough and move forward spiritually.

People in leadership, or in any positions for that matter, should not be afraid to pray the psalmist's prayer found in Psalm 139:23-24: "Search me, O God, and know my heart; test me and know my thoughts. Point out anything in me that offends you, and lead me along the path of everlasting life."

In this way, people who lead others by godly example can develop godly character before they step into leadership roles.

Godly Character

Character—good or bad—cannot be hidden for long. Eventually it will surface for everyone to see. Those with whom we associate influence our character. Solomon noted, **As iron sharpens iron, so one man sharpens another** (Prov. 27:17 NIV). Of course, we don't always have the luxury of choosing our associates, but we can choose our friends.

A good way to test whether or not we've chosen good friends is to ask ourselves, "Are these people causing me to grow, or are they pulling me down?" If our friends are pulling us down, then we need to carefully leave those relationships. However, if a spouse is pulling us down, we should spend time praying for a positive change and spend extra time demonstrating God's love to him or her.

Sometimes people build walls that prevent others from getting too close. Oftentimes people build these walls because of unresolved issues. Being unable to share is a harmful fear that Satan can use to hinder people and keep them from getting close to God or their friends.

Think again of the story of the prodigal son in Luke 16. After he had spent all of his money, alienated himself from his friends and found himself living in a pigsty, he finally remembered, *I can go home.*

Like the prodigal son, we should never allow shame to keep us from coming home to God. And, like the prodigal's father, God is always watching and waiting for our return should we stray from His fellowship.

God's interest is always in molding our character, making us into His image. Moses understood this when he wrote about the wilderness wanderings of the Israelites: "Remember how the

Lord your God led you through the wilderness for forty years, humbling you and testing you to prove your character, and to find out whether or not you would really obey his commands." (Deut. 8:2.)

Although the things we do may be hidden from others, they cannot be hidden from God. The Bible says, **The eyes of the Lord are in every place, beholding the evil and the good** (Prov. 15:3). Sooner or later everyone's character will reveal itself.

Ministers often tell people to focus on practicing the principles found in God's Word. What ministers do *not* usually tell people is that godly principles work only for the obedient. God is not bound to honor the efforts of the disobedient. The Word says, **"If you are willing and obedient, you shall eat the good of the land; but if you refuse and rebel, you shall be devoured by the sword"; for the mouth of the Lord has spoken** (Isa. 1:19,20 NKJV).

We will never apprehend God's high calling for us unless we willingly and obediently deal with any unresolved issues in our hearts. If we know what to do and refuse to do it, we are sinning. "Remember, it is sin to know what you ought to do and then not do it." (James 4:17.)

Harboring unresolved issues is not a modern-day mistake. Men throughout the Bible made this mistake. Look at the life of King David, for example, a man after God's own heart, according to the Scriptures. He had everything: the kingdom, prosperity, honor, wives, concubines, children, a supportive family and staff. One afternoon, however, something unexpected happened. Second Samuel 11:2-17 describes it.

Late one afternoon David got out of bed after taking a nap and went for a stroll on the roof of the palace. As he looked out over the city, he noticed a woman of unusual beauty taking a bath. He sent someone to find out who she was, and he was told, 'She is Bathsheba, the daughter of Eliam and the wife of Uriah the Hittite.'

Then David sent for her; and when she came to the palace, he slept with her. (She had just completed the purification rites after having her menstrual period.) Then she returned home.

When Bathsheba discovered that she was pregnant, she sent a message to inform David. So David sent word to Joab: "Send me Uriah the Hittite."

When Uriah arrived, David asked him how Joab and the army were getting along and how the war was progressing. Then he told Uriah, "Go on home and relax." David even sent a gift to Uriah after he had left the palace.

But Uriah wouldn't go home. He stayed that night at the palace entrance with some of the king's other servants.

David, a man who had pleased God, had gotten distracted by sin; he didn't know what he was in for but was desperate to keep his sin from being revealed.

When David heard what Uriah had done, he summoned him and asked, "What's the matter with you? Why didn't you go home last night after being away for so long?"

Uriah replied, "The Ark and the armies of Israel and Judah are living in tents, and Joab and his officers are camping in the open fields. How could I go home to wine and dine and sleep with my wife? I swear that I will never be guilty of acting like that."

"Well, stay here tonight," David told him, "and tomorrow you may return to the army." So Uriah stayed in Jerusalem that day and the next. Then David invited him to dinner and got him drunk. But even then he couldn't get Uriah to go home to his wife. Again he slept at the palace entrance.

So the next morning David wrote a letter to Joab and gave it to Uriah to deliver. The letter instructed Joab, "Station Uriah on the front lines where the battle is fiercest. Then pull back so that he will be killed." So Joab assigned Uriah to a spot close to the city wall, where he knew the enemy's strongest men were fighting. And Uriah was killed along with several other Israelite soldiers.

This is a sad description of David, a godly man, who stepped across the line and let lust control his actions. Instead of repenting, David tried to cover his sin by using murder and deceit.

Although David could hide these sins for a while, he could not remove them. These unresolved issues then nestled into David's conscience and went to work torturing him.

When Bathsheba heard that her husband was dead, she mourned for him. When the period of mourning was over, David sent for her and brought her to the palace, and she became one of his wives. Then she gave birth to a son. But the Lord was very displeased with what David had done. (2 Sam. 11:26,27.)

God is never pleased when we do not follow His principles. The Bible says, **Do not be deceived: God cannot be mocked. A man reaps what he sows. The one who sows to please his sinful nature, from that nature will reap destruction** (Gal. 6:7,8 NIV).

David married Bathsheba and probably thought he had everything taken care of. In other words, he seemed to be getting away with his sin. Months passed, and no one found out what had really happened, until one day God sent the prophet Nathan to David with a creative message.

Through Nathan, God told David this story: There were two men in a certain town. One was rich, and one was poor. The rich man owned many sheep and cattle. The poor man owned nothing but a little lamb he had worked hard to buy. He raised that little lamb, and it grew up with his children. It ate from the man's own plate and drank from his cup. He cuddled it in his arms like a baby daughter.

One day a guest arrived at the home of the rich man. But instead of killing a lamb from his own flocks for food, he took the poor man's lamb and killed it and served it to his guest.

David was furious. "As surely as the Lord lives," he vowed, "any man who would do such a thing deserves to die! He must repay four lambs to the poor man for the one he stole and for having no pity."

Then Nathan said to David, *"You are that man!* The Lord, the God of Israel, says, 'I anointed you king of Israel and saved you from the power of Saul. I gave you his house and his wives and the kingdoms of Israel and Judah. And if that had not been enough, I would have given you much, much more. Why, then, have you despised the word of the Lord and done this horrible deed? For you have murdered Uriah and stolen his wife. From this time on, the sword will be a constant threat to your family because you have despised me by taking Uriah's wife to be your own. Because of what you have done, I, the Lord, will cause your own household to rebel against you. I will give your wives to another man, and he will go to bed with them in public view. *You did it secretly, but I will do this to you openly in the sight of all Israel.'"*

Then David confessed to Nathan, "I have sinned against the Lord."

Nathan replied, "Yes, but the Lord has forgiven you, and you won't die for this sin. But *you have given the enemies of the Lord great opportunity to despise and blaspheme him."* (2 Sam. 12:13,14.)

"Thou art the man!" God's accusation hung heavy in the air before an astonished David. Immediately David confessed, but the damage to his family had already been done. He had given place to the devil, violating God's law, **Neither give place to the devil** (Eph. 4:27).

Shortly thereafter, everything changed for David's family. First, Bathsheba's child died (2 Sam. 12:15-18). Next, David's son Amnon raped his half-sister Tamar (2 Sam. 13:1-14). Two years later Tamar's brother, Absalom, had Amnon killed (2 Sam. 13:23-32). Shortly after that Absalom revolted (2 Sam. 15) and was later murdered by Joab, David's nephew and commander-in-chief (2 Sam. 18:15).

David himself had to go into exile during Absalom's revolt (2 Sam. 15-18), and Joab, who held the second highest position in the nation, became increasingly difficult to control. Ahithophel, one of David's trusted counselors and the grandfather of Bathsheba, joined Absalom's conspiracy, urging Absalom to take over David's harem (2 Sam. 15), which was symbolic of usurping all of David's authority. And finally, Adonijah, Bathsheba's other son, attempted to usurp the kingdom that had been promised to Solomon (1 Kings 1:9,25).

David, the man after God's own heart, repented of his adulterous liaison with Bathsheba and his involvement in the murder of Uriah. Thus, David was forgiven by God and told he would not die.

It would have been best for David to run to God at the first sign of temptation. Failing that, it would have been better for David to repent immediately after he sinned with Bathsheba than to go deeper into sin by deceiving and murdering Uriah.

Like David, people often think their sin is not hurting anyone but themselves, but that simply is not true. Unresolved issues and hidden sin hurt us and those we love. That's why it is vital to maintain a clean conscience before God.

Chapter 50

Lay Yourself and Your Ambitions on the Altar

Going into ministry requires a lot of prayer, self-examination and commitment to a life of servitude. Being effective in the ministry is definitely not easy, but it's possible when you do it step-by-step with God's help. And the first step is to lay yourself and your ambitions on the altar.

The apostles served in a secondary position to Jesus. In other words, they recognized Jesus' authority over them. That's one of the reasons they were called disciples. To be a disciple, one must be teachable and a follower after Jesus Christ, the Master.

Now, I would certainly never want to compare the position of senior pastor to that of Jesus Christ, but serving as an associate in any position does illustrate what it is like to be a disciple.

Let's look at the requirements Jesus laid down for discipleship. First, He required that the original disciples put God first. He said:

> If any man come to me, and hate not his father, and mother, and wife, and children, and brethren, and sisters, yea, and his own life also, he cannot be my disciple. And whosoever doth not bear his cross, and come after me, cannot be my disciple.
>
> Luke 14:26,27

The next thing Jesus required of His original disciples was that they renounce everything that was secondary to the Gospel. "Whoever does not renounce all that he has cannot be My disciple." (Luke 14:33.)

To renounce something means that you relinquish all claims to it. So when you renounce all you have, you place it in God's hands to be used or disposed of at His discretion. In other words, you surrender every part of your life to His lordship.

The final thing Jesus required of His original disciples was that they acknowledge Him as Lord of all.

I love a story I once read in a book called *The Man God Uses* by Dr. Oswald J. Smith. According to Dr. Smith, there was a preacher named Dr. Graham Scroggie, of Edinburgh, Scotland, who was speaking one time about repentance and coming back to the Lord. At the close of his service, a young woman who had been greatly stirred by his message approached him. She was a professing Christian, but she had resisted God's call on her life.

"Why don't you yield?" inquired Dr. Scroggie.

"I'm afraid I would have to do two things if I did," responded the woman.

"What are they?" questioned the minister.

"Well, I play the piano in a concert hall, and I fear I would have to give it up," explained the woman.

"And the other?"

"I'm afraid God would send me to China as a missionary."

Dr. Scroggie was wise in his dealings with the anxious woman. Opening his Bible to Acts 10:14, he read to her the passage in which Peter said to Jesus, **Not so, Lord.** Dr. Scroggie explained the absurdity of Peter's answer to the young woman.

"A slave never dictates to his master," Dr. Scroggie told her. "Therefore, to say, 'Not so,' and then add the word 'Lord,' is contradictory.

"Now," said Dr. Scroggie, "I want you to cross out the two words, 'Not so,' and leave the word 'Lord'; or cross out the word 'Lord' and leave the words 'not so.'"

After handing her a pencil, he quietly walked away.

For two hours she struggled, and then he returned. As he approached, he looked over her shoulder and saw a tear-stained page. On the page were the crossed-out words "Not so."

Later, the woman left with a beaming countenance. All the way home she repeated the word Lord over and over.

That woman would no longer dictate to her Master. Instead, she became His disciple, and He her Lord. Henceforth, it would be with her, "Even so, Father," and, "Lord, what wilt Thou have me to do?" (Acts 10:14).[1]

That's what laying everything on the altar means for all of us. Our relationships are strengthened when we make Jesus Lord of our lives, because we pass all emotional responses through Him first and then He can correct our perspective if necessary.

PART X

Recognize and Treasure a Good Relationship

Chapter 51

How To Recognize and Treasure a Good Relationship

In this book I've outlined nine ways to build a lasting relationship. Let me list them again below.

1. Develop a friendly lifestyle.

2. Fix yourself first.

3. Communicate, communicate, communicate.

4. Tip in advance.

5. Learn the difference between giving and receiving.

6. Control your expectations.

7. Guard your emotions.

8. Avoid attitudes that kill relationships.

9. Strengthen your relationship with God and the church.

By now, you should know that relationship-killing behavior stems from selfishness. In fact, no relationship can withstand a continual onslaught of the sins of self; namely, self-pity, self-righteousness, self-only interest, self-only protection and self-importance. Each of these can quickly turn to pride and arrogance. However, if you're willing to crucify the flesh and the sins of self by following the nine steps above, you can enjoy a lifetime of lasting, enriching relationships.

There are many ways to evaluate your relationships to determine whether or not they're good. Perhaps you already have a list started. But in case you still need help identifying the good qualities in relationships, here are a few characteristics to look for:

1. Both parties should feel comfortable with the relationship.
2. A positive, uplifting quality should be present during time spent together.
3. Each person should feel enriched for having known the other.
4. Neither time nor distance should cause the relationship to deteriorate.
5. Neither person should feel a need to behave falsely, sabotage, criticize or judge the other.
6. Each person should be honest with the other.
7. It should be easy to trust one another.
8. Both parties should be motivated by a willingness to forgive and forget past mistakes.

Lasting relationships require a lot of care and work. But we can enjoy them if we're willing to follow the example of the pearl merchant in Matthew 13:45-46: **Again, the kingdom of heaven is like unto a merchant man, seeking goodly pearls: who, when he had found one pearl of great price, went and sold all that he had, and bought it.**

By placing a high priority on our relationships with others and investing a lot of hard work and caring, we can live the kind of life God desires for us—one filled with a closeness to and love for others.

I hope you're encouraged to invest time and energy into your godly friendships. I encourage you to begin cultivating and rebuilding those special relationships with the people closest and most dear to you, especially those within your own household. When you do that, you can enrich your life immeasurably and find yourself happier than you've ever imagined you could be.

Endnotes

Foreword

[1] Debra Baker, "Beyond Ozzie and Harriet," *ABA Journal*, (Chicago: Copyright American Bar Association, September 1998).

[2] William A. Galston, Divorce American Style," *Public Interest*, No. 124, Summer 1996, 14.

[3] Barna Research Group, Ltd., *Barna Research Online*, 21 December 1999, <http://www.barna.org/cgi-bin/MainTrends.asp> (1 September 2000).

Chapter 1

[1] Bergen Evans, *Dictionary of Quotations*, (New York: Delacorte, 1968), 254.3.

[2] *The Living Bible*, 1 Corinthians 13:4-8:

> Love is very patient and kind, never jealous or envious, never boastful or proud, never haughty or selfish or rude. Love does not demand its own way. It is not irritable or touchy. It does not hold grudges and will hardly even notice when others do it wrong. It is never glad about injustice, but rejoices whenever truth wins out. If you love someone you will be loyal to him no matter what the cost. You will always believe in him, always expect the best of him and always stand your ground in defending him. All the special gifts and powers from God will someday come to an end, but love goes on forever.

Chapter 2

[1] Ted Engstrom, with Robert C. Larson, *The Fine Art of Friendship*, (Nashville: Thomas Nelson). This book is an excellent source of information on building friendships. As a result of reading this book, I carried four basic ideas around in my subconscious for quite some time before they found their way, reworked and presented from my own point of view, into four chapters in this book. Those chapters are "Nurture a Real Interest in Others," "Treat All People as Equals," "Be There in Triumph and Tragedy" and "Demand Nothing in Return."

[2] Harvey MacKay, *Swim With the Sharks Without Being Eaten Alive.* (New York: Ivy, 1988), 25-34.

[3] Bergen Evans, 396.7.

Chapter 3

[1] *The Oxford Dictionary of Quotations,* 3d ed. (Oxford: Oxford University Press, 1980), 232.8.

Chapter 5

[1] Louis H. Evans, Jr. *Creative Love,* (Old Tappan, NJ: Flemming H. Revell, 1977), 34-36. The author identifies these eight covenants out of the Word of God. The entire book is an outstanding discussion of these covenants.

[2] Bergen Evans, 710.5.

Chapter 6

[1] Josh McDowell, *The Secret of Loving,* (San Bernadino, CA: Here's Life, 1985), 88.

Chapter 7

[1] Bergen Evans, 551.5.

[2] J.E. Orr, *Prayer, Its Deeper Dimensions,* (London: Marshall, Morgan & Scott, 1963), 21.

[3] *The Oxford Dictionary of Quotations,* 535.26.

Chapter 11

[1] W.E. Vine, *An Expository Dictionary of New Testament Words,* (Lynchburg, VA: The Old-Time Gospel Hour), 499-500.

[2] Ibid., 1134.

Chapter 13

[1] Margery Williams, *The Velveteen Rabbit,* (New York: Avon, 1975), 12.

[2] Ibid., 12-16.

[3] E.M. Griffin, *Making Friends (& Making Them Count),* (Downer's Grove, IL: Inter Varsity, 1987), 28-29.

[4] Ibid., 30-36.

[5] Ibid.

6   Ibid., 36-41.

7   *The Oxford Dictionary of Quotations*, 430.19.

Chapter 14

1   Oswald J. Smith, *The Man God Uses*, (London: Marshall, Morgan & Scott, 1962), 21-28.

2   David Wilkerson, *The Refiner's Fire*, Vol. 1. (Lindale, TX: World Challenge), 80.

Chapter 16

1   Denis Waitley, *Seeds of Greatness: The Ten Best-Kept Secrets of Total Success.* (Pocket Books, 1986).

2   McDowell, 147.

3   Waitley.

Chapter 19

1   Vine, 933.

2   Ibid., 452.

Chapter 24

1   John Malloy.

2   Griffin, 94.

Chapter 30

1 M. Scott Peck, M.D., *The Road Less Traveled*, (New York: Simon and Schuster, 1978), 116.

Chapter 36

1 L.J. DuBois, *Life's Intimate Friendships*, (Anderson, IN: Warner), 53-54.

Chapter 38

1   Paul D. Meier, M.D.; Frank B. Minirth, M.D.; and Frank B. Wichern, Ph.D., *Introduction to Psychology and Counseling*, (Grand Rapids, MI: Baker, 1982), 85.

2   Ibid., 86.

3   Ibid.

[4] Ibid.

[5] Ibid., 87.

[6] Ibid.

[7] Ibid.

[8] Ibid.

[9] Ibid.

[10] Ibid.

[11] Ibid.

[12] Ibid., 88.

Chapter 40

[1] Vine, 446-447.

Chapter 45

[1] Charles Dickens, *David Copperfield.*

Chapter 50

[1] Smith, 47-48.

References

Baker, Debra. "Beyond Ozzie and Harriet." *ABA Journal*.

Barna Research Group, Ltd., *Barna Research Online*, 21 December 1999, http://www.barna.org/cgi-bin/MainTrends.asp> (1 September 2000). Chicago: Copyright American Bar Association, September 1998.

Dickens, Charles. *David Copperfield*.

DuBois, L.J. *Life's Intimate Friendships*. Anderson, IN: The Warner Press.

Engstrom, Ted, with Robert C. Larson. *The Fine Art of Friendship*. Nashville: Thomas Nelson.

Evans, Bergen. *Dictionary of Quotations*. New York: Delacorte, 1968.

Evans, Louis H., Jr. *Creative Love*. Old Tappan, NJ: Flemming H. Revell, 1977.

Galston, William A. "Divorce American Style," *Public Interest*. No. 124, Summer 1996.

Griffin, E.M. *Making Friends (& Making Them Count)*. Downer's Grove, IL: Inter Varsity, 1987.

MacKay, Harvey. *Swim With the Sharks Without Being Eaten Alive*. New York: Ivy, 1988.

Malloy, John.

McDowell, Josh. *The Secret of Loving*. San Bernadino, CA: Here's Life, 1985.

Meier, Paul D., M.D.; Minirth, Frank B., M.D.; and Wichern, Frank B., Ph.D. *Introduction to Psychology and Counseling, Christian Perspectives and Applications*. Grand Rapids, MI: Baker, 1982.

Orr, J.E. *Prayer, Its Deeper Dimensions*. London: Marshall, Morgan & Scott, 1963.

The Oxford Dictionary of Quotations, 3d ed. Oxford: Oxford University Press, 1980.

Peck, M. Scott, M.D. *The Road Less Traveled*. New York: Simon and Schuster, 1978.

Smith, Oswald J. *The Man God Uses*. London: Marshall, Morgan & Scott, 1962.

Vine, W.E. *An Expository Dictionary of New Testament Words*. Lynchburg, VA: The Old-Time Gospel Hour.

Waitley, Denis. *Seeds of Greatness: The Ten Best-Kept Secrets of Total Success.* Pocket Books, 1986.

Wilkerson, David. *The Refiner's Fire,* Vol. 1. Lindale, TX: World Challenge.

Williams, Margery. *The Velveteen Rabbit.* New York: Avon, 1975.

About the Author

Don Clowers is an international evangelist, teacher, pastor and author. For over forty years, he has traveled throughout the world, ministering to thousands through his evangelistic crusades. He also leads ministers' conferences to equip pastors and church leaders for more effective ministry. He resides in Dallas with his wife Sharon.

To contact Don Clowers,
write

Don Clowers
Don Clowers Ministries
P.O. Box 3168
Coppell, Texas 75019

*Please include your prayer requests
and comments when you write.*

Other Books by Don Clowers

Spiritual Growth

Never Be a Victim Again

Never Be a Victim Again Study Guide

God's Prescription for Health and Healing

God's Prescription for Health and Healing Study Guide

Additional copies of this book
are available from your local bookstore.

Harrison House
Tulsa, Oklahoma 74153

Prayer of Salvation

A born-again, committed relationship with God is the key to the victorious life. Jesus, the Son of God, laid down His life and rose again so that we could spend eternity with Him in heaven and experience His absolute best on earth. The Bible says, For God so loved the world, that he gave his only begotten Son, that whosoever believeth in him should not perish, but have everlasting life (John 3:16).

It is the will of God that everyone receive eternal salvation. The way to receive this salvation is to call upon the name of Jesus and confess Him as your Lord. The Bible says, That if thou shalt confess with thy mouth the Lord Jesus, and shalt believe in thine heart that God hath raised him from the dead, thou shalt be saved. For whosoever shall call upon the name of the Lord shall be saved (Romans 10:9-10,13).

Jesus has given salvation, healing and countless benefits to all who call upon His name. These benefits can be yours if you receive Him into your heart by praying this prayer.

Father,

I come to you right now as a sinner. Right now, I choose to turn away from sin, and I ask you to cleanse me of all unrighteousness. I believe that your Son, Jesus, died on the cross to take away my sins. I also believe that He rose again from the dead so that I might be justified and made righteous through faith in Him. I call upon the name of Jesus Christ for salvation. I want Him to be the Savior and Lord of my life. Jesus, I choose to follow You, and ask that You fill me with the power of the Holy Spirit. I declare that right now, I am a born-again child of

God. I am free from sin, and full of the righteousness of God. I am saved in Jesus' name, Amen.

If you have prayed this prayer to receive Jesus Christ into your life, we
would like to hear from you. Please write us at:

Harrison House
P.O. Box 35035
Tulsa, Oklahoma 74153

The Harrison House Vision

Proclaiming the truth and the power
Of the Gospel of Jesus Christ
With excellence;

Challenging Christians to
Live victoriously,
Grow spiritually,
Know God intimately.